BARRY FARBER'S

GUIDE TO HANDLING SALES OBJECTIONS

CAREER
PRESS
Franklin Lakes, NJ

Copyright © 2005 by Barry Farber

BARRY FARBER'S GUIDE TO HANDLING SALES OBJECTIONS
EDITED AND TYPESET BY CLAYTON W. LEADBETTER
Cover design by Mada Design, Inc. / NYC
Printed in the U.S.A. by Book-mart Press

To order this title, please call toll-free 1-800-CAREER-1 (NJ and Canada: 201-848-0310) to order using VISA or MasterCard, or for further information on books from Career Press.

The Career Press, Inc., 3 Tice Road, PO Box 687,
Franklin Lakes, NJ 07417
www.careerpress.com

Library of Congress Cataloging-in-Publication Data

Farber, Barry J.
   Barry Farber's guide to handling sales objections / by Barry Farber.
      p. cm.
   Includes index.
   ISBN 1-56414-773-8 (paper)
      1. Selling. 2. Sales management. I. Title: Guide to handling sales objections. II. Title.

HF5438.25.F369 2005
658.85—dc22

                                                                    2004054533

To all the people who have dealt with the many objections in their careers but never gave up, despite them.

CONTENTS

INTRODUCTION

This is a book about handling objections, the one thing that many salespeople—especially those just starting out—fear the most. The purpose is not just to help beginning salespeople handle objections by following the steps and techniques included here, but to understand the entire process, to understand the bigger picture so that you know why customers bring up objections in the first place, and to understand how to eliminate many objections before they arise.

Many salespeople are afraid to hear a customer say no, so they don't ask the difficult questions, the ones that qualify this customer as being the decision-maker or having the budget to afford their product or service. They're afraid to ask for the order, because they might get an objection they don't know how to handle.

But mostly they're afraid because they don't want to face rejection (who does?). What they don't understand, and what this book will reveal, is that objections are really opportunities to move the sale beyond what the customer sees as a barrier.

It's this misunderstanding, this misperception of objections, that fuels the salesperson's fear. However, there are two things that I have learned in life that have helped me get through the rough times:

1. Fear can hold you back only if you let it.
2. Everyone faces rejections, setbacks, and adversity. You can't always avoid it, but you can learn from it and become better at what you do and who you are.

Facing the Fear of Objections

Someone once told me that "fear" is an acronym for the phrase "false evidence appearing real." Therefore, the first step in dealing with any fear is to face it head-on and analyze it, to find out what is real and what is not. As every horror fan knows, it's not the monsters we can see that are so scary—it's the unexplained sounds in the night, or the shadowy figure cloaked in darkness. When we don't know what's real and what's not, our imagination begins to work overtime. It's the unknown that frightens us.

You're stepping into the unknown every time you make a sales call. There is no way (no matter how many objection-handling techniques you learn) to guarantee the consequences. But there are ways of dealing with fear. Teddy Atlas, trainer to some of the best boxers in the business, put it this way, "Fear is like fire. When it's controlled, it'll cook for you, it will heat your home, it will do a lot of good things. When it's not controlled it will burn up everything around you, consume everything.

> "Courage is not the absence of fear, it is the conquest of it. Not until you dare to attack will you master your fears.
>
> —From *I Dare You!* by William H. Danforth

"Same with fear. When it's controlled, it will make you better. It will make you prepare.... It will make you do what you have to do to survive. And if it's not controlled it will consume you just like fire; it will destroy you. You have to understand fear is an ally, not an enemy."

Objections Are Not Rejections

Fear is not the only ally you have when making a sales call. Believe it or not, objections fall into that category as well. As you'll learn throughout this book, objections are actually the foundation upon which you build a sale, because they give you information about the customer's needs and concerns. Armed with that information, you can move forward to show the customer how your product or service can meet those needs.

Unfortunately, objections don't usually feel like helpful building blocks. They feel like rejections—personal and professional. But if you are going to be a successful salesperson, you must understand that objections come with the territory. I have been in sales for more than 25 years now, and I sell a lot of different things. I sell my services as a speaker and trainer; I sell my clients, as an agent for business leaders, entertainers, and athletes; and I sell and market products such as the FoldzFlat Pen, the world's only writing instrument that folds flat, smaller than a credit card. I experience rejection and objections every day. If you're in sales (in fact, if you're alive), you will experience objections, obstacles, setbacks, and rejection.

Life is a grindstone—it either grinds you down or polishes you up, an old saying tells us. The good news is that, each time we experience a setback or disappointment, we also gain new information. If we use that information and learn from it, we actually become stronger and more resilient. Obstacles attacked strengthen us for the next time. Failure leads to success as long as we're learning its lessons. We learn more from failures than we ever learn from our successes. We build inner strength and character when things are most devastating. Each time we run into obstacles or experience adversity, we can get through it, if we look for the lessons they provide.

The purpose of this book is not only to show you how to change objections into opportunities, but also to let you know that even the most successful salespeople have had to deal with objections and obstacles along the way. It's frustrating when things don't go as planned. This is something that inventors know very well. When Thomas Edison was inventing the electric light, he failed 1,200 times before he finally got it to work. A journalist asked him, "How did you deal with 1,200 failures?" Edison replied, "I did not fail 1,200 times. I was successful in finding 1,200 ways the light bulb didn't work."

Inventors expect failures; salespeople should expect objections. Every time an inventor's experiment "fails" he can eliminate materials or processes that stand in the way of the solution. Every time you face an objection, you have the opportunity to eliminate the concern that stands in the way of your solution.

Every successful salesperson has had to face his or share of adversity, objections, and "failed" sales. And every successful salesperson has learned to put fear and failure into proper perspective, to gain strength and knowledge from difficulty. Such salespeople use their setbacks—in fact, they benefit from them. They know that success only comes from repeated triumph over adverse conditions, and that obstacles conquered provide information for future attempts.

Everyone goes through rough times. Those who don't cope well with adversity get pulled down by its undertow and don't have the skills to swim back to shore. Not only that, they repeatedly enter the same waters, in the same spot, and are surprised when the undertow catches them again.

> "Not many people are willing to give failure a second opportunity. They fail once and it's all over. The bitter pill of failure...is often more than people can handle.... If you're willing to accept failure and learn from it, if you're willing to consider failure as a blessing in disguise and bounce back, you've got the potential harnessing of one of the most powerful success forces.
>
> —Joseph Sugarman, American businessman and entrepreneur

Successful salespeople, too, have been caught in the undertow of adversity. But they learn from their experience. They don't enter the same waters again. However, if they should somehow get swept under once more, they use skills they learned form their first experience to guide them back to solid ground.

There are two choices in life: You can dig a hole or you can build a mountain. Realize that you're shoveling either way. No one breezes through life. Everyone does his or her share of shoveling. What you end up with depends on you.

You can focus on the hole you're digging or on the mountain you're building. You can spend your life digging for the buried treasure, chasing after fool's gold, cheating and lying through the day. Or you can use each shovelful to build a solid foundation upon which you can build success. You are constructing your future from

> I have learned that success is to be measured not so much by the position one has reached in life as by the obstacles which he has overcome while trying to succeed.
>
> —Booker T. Washington, essayist and naturalist

the fundamentals you must consistently maintain, the day-to-day tasks that must be accomplished.

The hole represents shortcuts in life, instant gratification, not preparing for sales calls, not caring about your customers, short-term gains. The mountain represents honesty, effort, fundamentals, serving your customer's needs, long-term gains. When you're constantly digging holes, you'll suddenly find yourself falling into one. Even though it's harder to build a mountain, once you get to the top, you can be proud of what you've accomplished.

When you let fear and obstacles keep you from doing and being your best, you are constantly digging holes. When you build a mountain, however, each new shovelful is supported by the one beneath it. Suddenly you find yourself on top of the mountain, and it's huge. People may wonder how you climbed that high. You and you alone know how that mountain was built.

Most salespeople think that the worst-case sales scenario is when a customer throws an unexpected objection at you. The truth is, the worst-case scenario is when you hear nothing at all—when the customer just "fades away," doesn't return your phone calls, doesn't reply to your e-mails, cancels the meetings, and you never hear a word of explanation. You haven't made the sale and you don't know why. Chances are you'll never find out.

When a customer expresses an objection, what he or she is really saying is, "I can't buy your product or service because...." When that happens, you've got the greatest sales opportunity in the world. This customer has told you exactly what's holding up the buying decision. All you have to do now is show the customer how the product or service you're offering is not the problem he sees it to be, but instead can benefit him in a variety of ways.

Of course, that's a simplistic view of what happens in real-life sales. In real-life sales, people don't always tell you exactly what their objections are. You often have to dig deep to find them (by following the six-step method in the next chapter). And in real life, solutions to a customer's problems don't always come to you in a flash of immediate inspiration.

As you read further, you will learn about the most real-life objections salespeople hear, and you'll learn specific techniques for dealing with them. But there are four things to keep in mind when you're dealing with objections, whatever they might be.

1. **Objections are buying signals.** When a customer raises an objection, he or she is really saying, "I want to buy your product or service, but I want to get this one problem solved before I go ahead."

2. **Objections provide opportunities to better understand customers.** This includes understanding how they think, how they communicate, what their concerns are, where their priorities lie, and so on. These are all important clues that can help you form better relationships with your customers for immediate sales and for future sales, as well. Often, the one thing that gets you past barriers and through objections is the relationship that is formed between you and the customer.

3. **Objections come in many varieties.** An objection can be a simple request for missing information. An

objection can be a test by someone who wants to see how much you know (or don't know) about his business. It could be a negotiating ploy. An objection can be used to hide the customer's fear of making a mistake. An objection can be the customer's way of saying, "I just don't like you," without coming right out and saying it. It's your job to discover, through the techniques you'll find in the rest of this book, just what kind of objection you're really facing.

4. **Objections help you move on.** Once you have effectively handled an objection, it is time to move on to the next stage of the sales process. If you can't handle the objection, it may be time to move on to another customer (there is more about this in Chapter 9).

Eliminating Objections Before They Arise

Whenever I do a sales seminar or training session and get to the part about handling objections, people just go crazy. This is the part they've been waiting for all day. Everyone wants to jump up and say, "Oh boy, have I got one for you. What would you do if somebody gave you this objection..." or, "You wouldn't believe the objection I got the other day...." They can't wait to tell me how clever they were in answering the objection, or how disappointed they were because they couldn't get beyond the objection.

17

Unfortunately, most salespeople I see today are missing the bigger picture. They think that if only they can master *handling* objections, they'll be meeting their sales quota in no time. They believe (or they've even been taught) that handling objections is accomplished by manipulating the sales process in their favor.

Well, I'm here to tell you that the best, most effective way to handle objections has nothing to do with being clever, tricky, or manipulative. The best way to handle objections is to stop them from coming up in the first place, and that is accomplished through the preparation you do before you ever get to the sales call. There are three keys to eliminating objections before they arise:

1. **Learn everything there is to learn about your customer, his business, and his industry.** Customers want salespeople whose main goal is to understand them and their businesses. They want reps who spend time in pre-call planning so that they have basic information before they get there and who understand their total environments, their overall industries, and their main competitors. They want to know that the rep is interested in finding out about their goals and objectives (a good sales rep might even help the customer define those goals). You can eliminate a

large number of objections by developing a broad range of knowledge—knowledge of the customer's goals and environment, and knowledge of his own product and policies. Customers want to know that you will be able to provide solutions, eliminate headaches, and help them grow their business.

There are some sales reps who show up in front of a customer with five products they've brought in because their managers said, "I want you to push those products." Don't think you can just plop those products in front of the customer and get a "yes" on the spot. It's tempting to go for the quick sale, but you're better off making sure you understand the customer's goals and strategies and the big picture of what he's trying to do.

2. **Match a customer with the product or service that suits him best.** Once you've learned who a customer is and what his needs are, your goal is to accommodate those conditions. If your product doesn't qualify, you may have to walk away from that particular sale. But the only way you can know that for sure is to know your product inside and out.

That kind of knowledge enables you to pull information out when you are looking for solutions for

19

customers. You're able to say, "You mentioned that these two factors are most important to you. Well, here's how our product can meet your needs in those areas..." or "Here's how we can help you with this challenge and make it easier for you to...."

3. **Fulfill all the steps in the sales cycle.** The biggest reason objections arise is because the salesperson is trying to sell the wrong product to the wrong person at the wrong time. If you try to close a deal before you know if your customer even needs or wants your product or service, you'll automatically get an objection. If you try to make a sale before you've built a rapport and relationship with that customer, you're leaving yourself wide open. Once in a while, you may get lucky and sail through a sale with no problems at all. But in the long run, there are no shortcuts here. There's an old sales cliché that's true nonetheless: People do business with people they like, trust, and respect. You have to earn each one of those things from your customers.

This kind of preparation requires focus, concentration, and hard work. However, there is a basic truth of life that says what you put into it is what you get back. The rewards you get out of any endeavor depend on the amount of effort you put into it. Sometimes we're afraid of working hard, because we're afraid we won't get the reward in the end. Rewards are sometimes long in coming, but they do come. Most sales-people, who don't achieve as much success as they want to, don't fall short because of lack of ability, but because they gave up too soon or didn't put in 100-percent effort. Those who do achieve success know that it is only concentrated, focused effort that will produce results.

There May Be a Six-Step Method, But There's No One Way to Handle Objections

Although I am a salesperson (amongst other things) by trade, I am also a devotee of the martial arts. I earned a black belt in Tae Kwon Do, a linear art that teaches you to go after your opponent with strikes, kicks, and blocks. Then I studied aikido, a form in which you learn *not* to attack in a fight, but to counter the other person's moves, using his weight and energy against him. Now I am a student of jujitsu, which com-bines the principles and techniques of both aikido and Tae Kwon Do.

In selling, as in the martial arts, there are times when being aggressive is the only way to close the deal. At other times, a softer approach is the right one to take. The difference is that, in selling, our customers are not our enemies. They are,

21

instead, our sparring partners, and both of us should come out stronger in the end.

Leading With the "Soft" Sell

There are three "soft" steps you can take when someone comes at you with an objection:

1. **Listen and Observe.** You not only want to know what the person is saying to you, but how she's saying it as well. You want to hear the words, and analyze the personality behind the words. Most important, you want to establish eye contact, to create a bond that can lead to a strong relationship.

2. **Question.** You can't counter an attack unless you're able to size up your opponent; only then can you know what moves are possible for you to make next. You can't handle an objection unless you understand exactly what it is and where it's coming from. Only then can you see the possibilities available to make you and your product or service fit with your customers' needs. Question your customers' objections and ask them to explain, expand, and elaborate until you fully understand the situation.

3. **Present with a value-added response.** Based on the first two steps, you can now come back with a strong

tie-in: "You mentioned that this was your real concern about using this product. Here's what we can do for you to make sure your needs are met...." In this way, you can use your customers' own objections to deflect their concerns and lead them to positive resolutions of what they perceive as conflicts.

Follow With the "Hard" Sell, If Necessary

Sometimes in sales, as in the martial arts, it is necessary to take a more aggressive approach. There are two steps to follow here:

1. **Let your enthusiasm and passion show.** Let your customers see that you believe strongly that there is a match between what they need and what you've got to offer. There's a saying in martial arts, "If you understand yourself and not your opponent, you win half the battles. If you understand your opponent and not yourself, you win half the battles. If you understand your opponent and yourself, you win 100 percent of the battles. If you understand neither, you win no battles." If you really understand yourself and what you're selling, and you really understand the customer, you will come away with a win-win situation.

2. **Have the backup to support your belief.** In sales, belief and enthusiasm can carry the day—only if it is backed up by knowledge and understanding. Have all your facts and figures down, and have at least three or four strong reasons your product is different and stands out from the rest.

The most important techniques in martial arts are those that teach you how to get hit and how to fall, when you're surprised by an opponent, so that you can get back up with even greater strength. When you're trying to make a sale, you have to know what to do when an objection comes at you from left field. You have to be ready and able to use what you've learned about your customer, what you know about yourself and your product, and how much you believe in what you're doing to make the strongest close.

A Real-Life Example

I am selling every day, in one way or another. I have probably heard every objection that has ever been invented. So, whenever I can, I use the six-step method to handle the objections that arise. I also know that there are situations that just don't fit into a tidy little box and cannot be handled in a linear, one-through-six fashion.

Recently, for instance, I was representing a well-known, established entertainer who wanted to get on radio. He didn't really have any experience in this area. Stations were naturally hesitant to take a chance on someone who'd never done his own show before. This was an objection I heard from several station owners, and I had to find a way to come up with a value-added solution that would satisfy both the station owners and my entertainment client.

So I came up with a plan: I offered the entertainer's services to take over a spot when one of the station's top hosts went on vacation. I also brought in one of my corporate clients to sponsor these shows. So the station got someone to fill in for one of its most popular hosts, complete with sponsor, and my entertainment client got a chance to use these shows as demos for all the other syndicated markets.

Sometimes the best way to deal with objections is to use creative solutions. There are exceptions to all rules; as the great martial artist Bruce Lee said, "the only way is no way." But you can't break out of the box unless you have a solid foundation beneath you. That's why you need to learn the six-step method and all the other techniques in this book.

Most important, however, is to realize that you cannot learn everything you need to know about handling objections by reading this book—or any other book on the subject. The only way to learn is go out and sell. Take action. Take a risk. There is no guarantee you will succeed at everything you try; the only guarantee is the failure that comes with never having tried at all.

The most important lesson you can take away from this chapter is one that may surprise you and one that I will repeat over and over again in this book: **This six-step method doesn't always work.** What I mean is, you can't memorize these six steps and expect to use them verbatim in every situation to close every sale. Sometimes you won't need all six steps. You do the first two, you clear up the objection and— badda bing, badda boom—you're on to the close. On the other hand, if you're selling a high-ticket item and you have a very long sales cycle, you may end up using all six steps and then some.

The six steps are your base, the foundation upon which you build your selling skills. Learn these six steps and you will be way ahead of the game. But don't be fooled into thinking that these six steps will be all you'll ever need. Before we get to the six steps, here are some other tips, hints, and techniques that will help you become a more effective salesperson:

◆ **Sell what you believe in.** If you're reading this book to learn how to sell a product you don't believe in, you might as well close the cover right now. You can still learn how to handle objections, and you will probably make some sales, but you will never be a truly successful salesperson. Why don't you believe in the product you're selling? Is it not going to perform for the customer? Is the product something that is being sold without integrity? If so, no amount of skill will enable you to get past the objections you will run into. If you don't believe in yourself, your product, or your service, you will never get your customer to believe in you. And that's what it really comes down to in the end. The best way to handle objections is to help your customers believe in you, and believe that you are looking out for their best interests.

◆ **Have faith.** The great American author and storyteller Mark Twain once said, "Fear came knocking at the door. Faith answered and no one was there." The same can be said of objections: An objection came knocking at your door. Faith answered and no objection was there. When you have faith in yourself and your abilities, when you believe in your product or service strongly, you will find yourself having to face fewer and fewer objections. You have to believe absolutely in your heart that what you're doing has value, and that you're willing to work as hard as necessary to achieve your goals. If that faith in yourself is strong enough, it is communicated to those around you and they come to have faith in you (and your product or service) as well.

✦ **Really listen to your customers.** Have them speak from the heart. Find out what drives them, what gets them going, what gets them pumped on life. Ask, "What's important to you? What are your challenges today? What's the next step I need to do to earn your business?" Once you get them talking about what fires them up, what gets them going about their organization, and what visions they have for the future, you've made a lasting connection. When that happens, you build an incredibly strong bond that lessens the impact of any objections that may arise. You want them to share their challenges and goals—the real ones that your product can make an impact on. That makes it easy for you to say, "I understand what your challenges are and here's how we can help you meet them."

✦ **Don't rely solely on your "natural" sales skill.** This is a question I get all the time: Are good salespeople born, or are they made? It's true, some people may have more natural-born talent than others. But, as Jack LeHav, founder and CEO of Remarkable Products, once told me, "Some people are born to be a 50-gallon barrel and some are born to be a 20-gallon barrel. What's important is that if you are born to be a 20-gallon barrel, make sure you fill up those 20 gallons. Don't be 20 gallons in a 50-gallon barrel."

It doesn't matter if you were born with 20 gallons worth of talent or 50, as long as you make the most of the abilities you have. I believe that anyone can be a successful salesperson, especially if he or she utilizes these three points:

❖ *Effort.* In the real world, there is only one secret to success. There is only one road—one long road—to follow to get to our goals. There are no shortcuts. Success comes from hard work. It comes from the extra effort we put in, from the work ethic we foster, and from the values to which we are committed. Only effort, sustained over time, will build the foundation to support success.

♦ *Patience and perseverance.* In our quest for instant gratification, we often forget two of the
most useful sales tools we can ever utilize: patience and perseverance. We have to plant seeds,
feed and water them, give them time to grow,
and then reap their harvest. You don't plant a
seed and expect a ripened crop the next day.
You must give the plant a chance to take root
and grow. At the same time, you cannot sit idly
by and wait for it to bear fruit. It takes care and
nurturing. Sales are the same way. You must
constantly be planting seeds every single day,
be patient when things are not proceeding as
quickly as you would like them to, and be persistent in your efforts to keep that sale alive and
flourishing.

♦ *Cultivated solutions.* Effort, patience, and persistence will not survive against objections unless you believe 100 percent that your product
or service has value and benefit for your customers. Do your research.

Talk to potential consumers and find out what
they do or do not like about your product or service. Ask them what they want it to do for them.

31

Talk to manufacturers and distributors of similar product lines. Use your research to get new ideas and to build on what you already have to offer. Test out your ideas. Find out what works and what doesn't.

If you get negative comments, remember what successful entrepreneur Famous Amos once said, "You can never sink a ship in any ocean unless you let the water inside." If you let others' doubts and negativity sink into your mind, you're done. After you've done as much research as you can, you can make intelligent choices about where your opportunities lie. Your belief in your product should be objective, not emotional. Only then will you be willing to put in the hard work and keep it going for as long as necessary.

If you have a 20-gallon barrel and you fill it to the brim, you're still way ahead of the game. If you make use of the three preceding elements—effort, patience and persistence, and cultivated solutions—you have what it takes to handle any objections that may come your way.

✦ **Start with the structure, and branch out from there.** Some people will tell you that the only skill you need to handle objections is to "be yourself." That's good advice, up to a point. However, many salespeople—especially beginning salespeople—take this to mean that they can go into a sales call and just wing it. That simply isn't true. You need a structure to give you a place to start, you need to know what questions to ask, you need to know the six steps for handling objections, and you need to have done your homework. Then you can use the greatest sales asset you will every own: your own personality.

When you have done your homework and when you are totally prepared for every sales call, you don't have to think so much about every little detail while you are there. You'll be able to sit back and sell from the heart.

When I was a sales manager, I had a rep who was not doing very well. At first, I

> There's a question that baseball great Yogi Berra once asked: "How can anybody think and hit at the same time?" My question is, "How can anybody think and sell at the same time?" The best salespeople are those who feel so comfortable with the sales process that they don't have to think about what they're doing. Selling is a natural extension of who they are.

couldn't understand his difficulty. He had a great personality; in fact, many people thought he was a natural-born salesperson. He had great rapport with everyone in the office and was very well liked. But he wasn't making the sales. So I went along with him on some sales to find out what the problem was. It didn't take long. As soon as we got in front of a customer, something happened to this rep's personality. It's as if he tucked his true self away in his pocket, and another person came out of his mouth. He was taking the customer through a robotic "by-the-book" sale straight out of Selling 101. He stepped into what he perceived to be the "salesperson mode" and stepped right out of the sale.

The best relationship you can have with a client is when you can simply be yourself. When you feel most comfortable with clients, they feel most comfortable with you. And that's when people *really* buy.

✦ **Continuous improvement.** Once you have mastered the foundations of your craft, continue to learn. Albert Einstein's greatest frustration in life was that no matter how deep he dug, no matter how much he studied, he could never come up with a definitive answer. There is always more to be discovered. This may be frustrating, but it's also exciting. It means there are endless possibilities in the world. The more you learn, the better you learn to sell. The continuous improvement in yourself is what constantly builds a better sales product, which is *you.*

✦ **Create a sense of urgency.** The most successful salespeople have the ability to keep the sale moving forward by conveying a sense of urgency. They don't just sit back and wait for the sale to take its course; they continually ask, "What is our next step?" in order to get the customer to move forward or to move in a new direction. Having a sense of urgency also topples some of the more trivial objections that are really requests for more information rather than true obstacles to the sale.

✦ **Manage your ego.** Everybody has an ego. That can be a good thing, unless it gets in the way of understanding the situation from the customer's point of view. We've all let our egos get involved in the conversation once in a while. An objection comes up, and no matter what it is—to our product, to our service, or because of our competition—we get so caught up in defending ourselves and fighting to prove that we are right that we forget our purpose in being there. We put ourselves first, and leave the customer behind. It isn't until we put ego aside that we can step back and truly listen to the customer's concerns.

✦ **Change your focus.** Sometimes you've got to change your focus to let the answer resolve itself. In other words, there are times when we get so focused on one objection—it might be a major objection, it might be a minor objection, it might not even be an objection at all, just a stall thrown at us—but we become so focused on that one objection we don't realize there are other avenues to look at. We have to stop what we're doing and take a look at the big picture. What is it you're really trying to accomplish? What the best way to go about it? How big of an obstacle is the objection? Where can we go to get help dealing with this objection? Sometimes the best idea is simply to stop trying to solve this puzzle for a while and move on to another task. Give yourself a mental break. More than likely, an answer will come to you when you least expect it.

✦ **Before you fix the problem, fix the customer.** Sometimes an objection is really nothing more than a complaint from a customer who wants to get something off his chest. Perhaps he had a bad experience with your company in the past, or with a competitor's product that's similar to yours. There are customers who don't want you to just fix their problem—at least not until they've said their piece. What's the best advice for dealing with these kinds of tough customers?

Put yourself in their shoes. Create empathy with statements such as, "I understand how you feel." Listen to their concerns without interruption. Don't argue with them or get angry or frustrated. We all have the same fears, anxieties, and egos; they're part of who we are. Your best bet is to get as much information as you can, to understand each and every customer as an individual, and to adapt your objection-handling techniques to each situation accordingly. It's the only way to turn tough customers into your best customers.

✦ **It's easier when you both win.** The ideal resolution to any problem situation is when both parties win, when there's a give and take. For instance, if there's a price objection, perhaps you can come up with compromise over a limited time period. You could say, "Here's what I'd like to do. I will sell you my product for this price for the first four months. By that time, you will be able to see the sell through and determine how much profit you can make. After four months, my price will go up to our current rate." In this way, you both win. The customer gets a lower price for a certain time period, and you eventually get your full asking price. This is the kind of win-win solution that builds long-lasting relationships.

✦ **Become unconsciously competent.** There are four stages of competence in any pursuit. When you begin a new skill, such as selling, you're unconsciously incompetent—you're not really aware of what you need to do to be effective. Eventually, as your skill improves, you become consciously incompetent—you know there's much more to learn and that you need to make improvements. Then, when you gain experience and start making more and more sales, you become consciously competent—you're aware of the steps you're taking and the things you're doing well. The last step, and the most important, is when you become unconsciously competent—you're so thoroughly skilled that you no longer have to think on a technical level, and that allows you to sell straight from heart.

That was Shakespeare's advice on how to be successful in the world: Never forget who you are; never try to be anyone other than the person you were meant to be. William Danforth, founder of Ralston Purina, had similar advice. He said, "Be your own self, at your very best, all the time." Not an easy assignment, but one that pays off in the end.

❖ *Be your own self...* That's what selling is all about. People want to feel confident that they made the right decision when buying your product. That confidence comes from the trust you provide when you build personal connections with your customers.

❖ *...at your very best...* Preparation is the key. Understand your customers' needs and challenges, and keep your objectives in mind at every call. Trust yourself enough to let your customers see who you are as a person, and they will return that trust to you.

❖ *...all the time.* Don't be like the young sales rep who had a split personality—one for "real" and one for "sales." Let your best asset shine through.

39

When you hide yourself, you hide your most valuable sales tool: you.

The Six-Step Method

You cannot become a great salesperson by reading from a script: I say this, then the customer says that, then I answer with this.... In real life, customers surprise you all the time. They never say what you want them to say or what you expect them to say.

> Prepare to get objections. Make a list of the most common objections you get with your product or service, your company, and/or your industry. Think about ways you've handled those objections in the past, what worked for you and what didn't. Find out how others in your company or industry handle similar objections. Then use those successes as a basis for handling similar objections that arise for you.

Then why bother with the six steps at all? Because they are guidelines, insights on how to structure your answers when objections arise. The concepts are sound, and should be used as the foundation upon which you build your skill and utilize your own creativity and talent in adapting them to your particular product or service and industry. There's no way I could write a book that would tell you exactly what to say in every situation; how you handle an objection if you're selling jet engines is going to be very different from how you handle an objection if you're selling donuts. But there are certain skills, such as listening to the entire objection, that fit every industry and every sales situation.

Once you learn the six steps and begin to use them in real life situations, experience will teach you how to use them most effectively.

The six steps are:

1. Listen to the objection in its entirety.
2. Define the objection.
3. Rephrase the objection into a question.
4. Isolate the objection.
5. Present the solution.
6. Close.

Step Number 1: Listen to the Objection in Its Entirety

Most people think they are good listeners. Most salespeople think they are great listeners. Yet one of the biggest complaints in relationships—both personal and professional— is that people don't really listen to one another. In fact, a survey quoted in the September 1999 issue of *Training and Development* found that 80 percent of responding executives rated listening as the most important skill in the workplace, and 28 percent rated listening as the skill most lacking in the workplace.

So why don't we listen more? One reason is that we have a sense of urgency to express ourselves. Salespeople, in particular, feel certain that if they could just express themselves convincingly, they would get the customer to see things their way. And they feel that talking is the best way to do that. They only half listen to what the customer is saying because they're so busy getting ready for the moment when they can jump in and talk the customer into the sale.

> " Mans inability to communicate is a result of his failure to listen effectively, skillfully, and with understanding to another person.
> —Carl Rogers, psychologist "

The result is that we miss all kinds of information. We interrupt. And then what happens? The customer gets annoyed, and often loses his train of thought, which is frustrating, to say the least. The customer then starts to ask himself, "Why is this salesperson getting so defensive?" or "This rep is not even listening to me. Why should I listen to her?"

Not to mention, if you start talking immediately, you're "answering" an objection before you're sure what it really is. I've been out on calls with many salespeople who think that, because they've just gone through a training session or because they're excited about a new feature of their product, they can just load the customer up with information and make the sale. Instead, what happens most often is that the sales rep ends up planting a whole new objection in the customer's head—one that he hadn't even thought about before!

What you're doing when you're really listening is practicing empathy—seeing things from the other person's point of view. Selling begins by putting yourself in the customer's shoes. The only way to find out what it's like to walk in those shoes is to listen carefully, to take notes when the customer is talking, to look him in the eye, and to nod your head,

> Nobody ever listened themselves out of a sale. An objection becomes an opportunity when we listen to the whole thing, hear it out, understand it, get the customer to expand on it, solve it, and move on.

to show him you understand what he's saying. Then pause for a few seconds before you begin to speak. Let the customer know you're considering how to answer, and you're not just going to tell him the same thing you've told dozens of other customers before.

Step Number 2: Define the Objection

You want to find out specifically what the customer is objecting to. Customers often say one thing and mean another. It's your job to get to the bottom of things, and you do so by asking for clarification, for more information about what is bothering the customer, and why. Convert vague objections into specific questions and statements. For instance, if a customer says, "I'm not sure I need that feature," ask, "Can you explain that to me?" or "Can you tell me why you feel that way?"

Another technique for getting customers to expand on their objections is what I call "Parroting." It's a more subtle way of getting people to expand their thoughts. A conversation might go:

>**Customer:** "I don't know if I'm comfortable with your service capabilities."
>
>**Rep:** "Comfortable?"
>
>**Customer:** "Well, I'm not sure your company is large enough to service all our locations."
>
>**Rep:** "Not large enough?"
>
>**Customer:** "Yes. The last company we used had problems getting to some of our branches...."

Now you know what the real objection is. He is worried that your company doesn't have the manpower for his service needs—a problem he had with other companies. Now you can answer with, "Then you'll be happy to know that we've recently added 10 new technicians to our service department and that our service extends throughout the tri-state area...." Of course, you

> You can get customers to define their objections by asking open-ended questions such as:
>
> ✦ "Can you expand on that?"
>
> ✦ "Can you elaborate on that?"
>
> ✦ "Tell me more about that...?"
>
> ✦ "Can you go into detail about...?"
>
> ✦ "Why is that?"
>
> ✦ "Can you explain what you mean by...?"

don't use this technique after every sentence, but it is a signal to the customer that you're really listening to what he's saying, and that you're interested to know more. The more you know, the more value you can add to your package.

Step Number 3: Rephrase the Objection Into a Question

Once you have gotten the customer to define the objection, you need to let the customer know that you listened to what she said, and that you understand her concern. At this point, she doesn't know if you've understood her, and you don't know if you've gotten to the bottom of the problem. Your objective in Step Three is to convert the objection into a question: "So based upon your projected sales, you want to be sure that we'll be able to supply you with inventory in a timely manner. Is that correct?"

> The best salespeople are simply those who understand that there is little difference between obstacles and opportunities and are able to turn both to their advantage.
>
> —Victor Kiam, American businessman and entrepreneur

You're restating the objection, not mimicking word for word what the customer has said. It's your understanding of the customer's problem, and if you have it right, you can go on to the next steps in the process. This is your opportunity to get back on track in case you have misunderstood what the customer needs.

Once again, you're creating empathy here. You're confirming that you understand what the problem is, and that this is an area you need to address with your product or service. When sales are lost, it's usually due to lack of communication and lack of clarification.

Step Number 4: Isolate the Objection

This step allows you to find out if the objection you just confirmed is the only one standing in the way of the sale.

So you might say, "All right. The ability of our service department to reach all your locations is the only thing that's keeping us from moving forward on this, is that right?"

Notice I said "moving forward." Many salespeople have been taught that their only objective is to get the customer to make the deal immediately and that if they don't, they have lost the sale. This may be true in rare cases, but for most customers, that kind of high pressure selling is a turn-off. Using a phrase like "moving forward" is a lot less threatening than "stopping us from making a decision today," or "stopping you from signing on the dotted line."

Not long ago, I went to a car dealership, but I didn't get very far. The saleswoman asked me a few basic questions and then began pushing. "So if I can find you just the car you're looking for at the right price, you'll make the purchase *today*, isn't that right?" No matter what I said, she kept coming back to that question, as if repeating the word *today* would make me buy the car. She never asked my name, never got to know anything about me or what I really needed. Had I been in market for a car, I never would have bought one from her. Obviously, she was trained in a certain technique and did not know how to deviate from her script.

This is not an effective way for a human to make a sale (maybe for a computer...). Nothing against qualifying, but do it without ticking your customers off.

You use this step for two reasons:

1. To be sure that once you have answered the concern the customer has expressed, no other objections are going to come up and stop you from moving on to the next step in the sales cycle.

2. So that you get everything on the table and out into the open. What customers respect most is that you're honest and straightforward with them at all times. They don't want any surprises later—and neither do you. You never want a customer to say, "Wait a minute. You never told me about this extra delivery charge for rush orders! Everything we do is a rush order!" When that happens, your trust has been broken, and you will have work doubly hard to get it back again.

Step Number 5: Present the Solution

Once you understand the customer's concern (and you and the customer have both agreed on that understanding), you can demonstrate how your product or service will fill that customer's needs. You can't proceed to Step Five until you have done the work required in the previous steps. You have to do your homework, learn about the customers, find out why they need your product or service, and determine what they are trying to accomplish. You need all this back-up information in order to make the best recommendation for that customer.

And remember, this step may not occur right on the spot. You may have to clarify the objection and then come back at another time with the solution. It could be that you have to speak with your manager, consult your partner, or ask for advice. For the best feedback, speak to at least three people. Tell them, "This is what I did, this is what the customer said, this is what happened, what would you do next?" If possible, call on three people with different backgrounds and different experiences. Then study the three suggestions you get and choose the one (or ones) that make the most sense to you. That feedback, plus your own evaluation of the situation, will provide you with a strong foundation to

> Sometimes it helps to take a step back and write out the objections and the possible solutions. Divide a page into the categories "customer's concern" and "possible solutions." Write out the positives, the negatives, the variables, the numbers involved, and the "what if we did this" scenarios. Often, just the act of putting it down on paper gives you a clearer answer on how to handle the situation. It's a way of collecting and organizing your thoughts to find the best possible answer.

move on to the next step and to increase your chances of making the sale—this time and in the future as well.

You have to be an expert in the elements of the sales cycle, outlined for you in Chapter 10, and you can find out more by reading *Superstar Sales Secrets* or *The 12 Clichés of Selling and Why They Work* (Workman Publishing Company, 2001), or by going to *www.barryfarber.com/artby/index.html* and reading some of the article you'll find there on the sales cycle.

Solutions don't come from thin air. You find solutions through qualifying and questioning. Really good questioning eliminates many objections before they arise. If your solution is going to be effective, it must be directly related to the customer's needs. If you know what your customer cares about most and direct your solution to that concern, you're well on your way to making the sale.

Step Number 6: Close

After you have presented your solution, it's time to close for the deal or close for the next step. It takes courage to close. You have to be strong and grounded. You have to be an expert in your field. You have to be a person who is committed to continuous improvement and to learning everything there is to know about your product, your service, your company, and your industry. That is what gives you the confidence to close. Confidence in action will allow you to go on past any periods of doubt you may have. When you know that you have truly listened to the customer, when you have asked questions to get to the customer's real needs, and

> When you're going after Moby Dick, bring the tarter sauce.

when you've presented a solution that addressed those needs, you're ready to close—and more than likely, the customer is ready to buy.

This is going to be short and sweet. It's also going to be a chapter of opposites. First, I'm going to tell you that "Feel, Felt, Found" is one of the most basic—and most applicable—methods of diffusing an objection that ever existed. It's one that can be used in almost any sales situation.

Next, I'm going to tell you not to use Feel, Felt, Found—at least, not in its exact form. It's one of those things that has become such a staple technique for handling objections that it has actually become a cliché. Not that it doesn't work; you just have to be careful how you use it.

I use it myself. I used it all the time in 1983 when I was selling newspaper advertising door to door. Here's how it went:

Objection example:

> ✧ "I'm sorry, but we don't buy newspaper advertising. We find it doesn't work for us."

Reply:

- ✧ "I can appreciate how you *feel*."
- ✧ "A lot of people I've spoken with *felt* that way too."
- ✧ "But when they *found* out how many people they could reach by advertising in our newspaper, they were amazed. I'd like to see if there's an opportunity to do the same for you. Would you be interested in a quarter page ad, or would a half page be better for you?"

NOTE: I have since learned that what should have been asked after hearing this objection is: "Why is that?" (step number 2 in the six-step method, as discussed in Chapter 2). After you fully understand the objection, you can go on to Feel, Felt, Found.

> Quick Feel, Felt, Found Tip:
>
> Don't pause after you say, "I'd like to see if we can do the same for you." Go directly into, "Would Thursday morning be good for you, or would the afternoon be better?"

This three-step method can actually be applied to just about any objection you might hear, by the gatekeeper or by anyone else you're dealing with. You just change the third part so that it applies to the particular objection. For example, if you were dealing with a price objection, you might say, "...when they *found* out how much money they saved by using our product (or service), they were amazed. I'd like to do the same for you. How is this Thursday morning for me to come in and talk to you about it? Or would the afternoon be better?"

Use It, Don't Abuse It

There's nothing wrong with using Feel, Felt, Found when it's appropriate. Just don't overuse it. Clearly, you can't use it to handle more than one objection in a sales call. Customers are a lot more savvy than they used to be, and many of them know about Feel, Felt, Found too.

In most cases, what you really want to do is ask questions to get your customers to reveal more about their objections. When you use Feel, Felt, Found, you never get beyond the surface of the objection and you're not addressing the deeper issues behind a customer's concerns.

This is another one of the "foundation" principles: Learn the Feel, Felt, Found method so well that you can use it without really using it. Find different ways to say it; adapt it any way that makes sense for your kind of sale.

In the next several chapters, you'll find the most common objections salespeople get and how to handle them. You can use the Feel, Felt, Found method with any type of objection.

Just remember that it is no substitute for asking questions, qualifying, and following all the other steps of the sales cycle. It's just another tool to keep in your objection-handling arsenal.

There is one thing that all salespeople have in common: They spend a tremendous amount of time trying to get in other people's doors (literally and figuratively). Getting in the door is often the greatest barrier you'll ever face. Once you're in and speaking to the decision-maker, you've got everything you've ever learned about sales, plus your own experience, to back you up. But none of this education will do you any good if you can't get in to see the person who has the ability to buy your product or service.

It really doesn't matter if you're prospecting for appointments on the phone or face-to-face. The objections, and the way you handle them, are the same. As a salesperson, there are two situations in which you'll find yourself when trying to get a foot in the door. One is when you first have to deal with a "gatekeeper" such as the company's receptionist, or the decision-maker's assistant. The second is when you are dealing with the decision-maker him- or herself.

Getting Past the Gatekeeper

There are some decision-makers who are notoriously hard to reach. Often, your best option is to make a connection with the gatekeeper. If you can make the gatekeeper your friend, you may succeed where others have failed, for three reasons: (1) the gatekeeper usually has inside information, (2) the gatekeeper often has "hidden" authority and power within the organization, and (3) the gatekeeper has the ability to spread the word about you and your product or service.

✦ **Form a relationship with the gatekeeper.** Remember that the gatekeeper is just doing his or her job; give that person the same respect you would give anyone else in the organization. It's building rapport that gets you in the door.

✦ **Articulate your praise and gratitude.** Gatekeepers are rarely recognized by salespeople (or many others in the office) for the help they have given. Let them know that you appreciate their help and advice. Send a handwritten thank-you note after you hang up, even if you haven't gotten an appointment. Then you can always call back and say, "I just wanted to be sure you got my note," and try for an appointment again. I once sent a note to a gatekeeper complimenting her on the great attitude she had with me on the phone. I called back three days later to follow up and she said, "You not only made my day, you made my week. Everyone here thinks I'm

> Quick Rapport-Building Tip:
>
> Send a handwritten thank-you note that's personalized to the gatekeeper. Include something you've discussed or something that relates specifically to the gatekeeper (see the example about the "attitude" note).

crabby so I showed them the note you sent and said, 'See?'" She then persuaded her boss to meet with me the following week.

✦ **Keep your sense of humor.** If you can get the gate-keeper to laugh, you're way ahead of the game. You don't need to be offensive or out-landish, but joking around a little can often get you a long way.

> Quick Rapport-Building Humor Tip:
>
> "I know you make all the decisions here—but can I speak to the person who thinks he makes all the decisions?"

✦ **Ask for his or her opinion.**

Objection example:

♦ "I'm sorry, but my boss isn't seeing any salespeople right now."

Reply:

♦ "I understand. However, I know that my product (or service) has tremendous value and would be of great help to your boss and your company. If you were in my position, what would you do?"

Feel, Felt, Found

Here's one situation where the Feel, Felt, Found system is an appropriate solution:

Objection example:

♦ "I'm sorry, but my boss is really busy now. He's not seeing any salespeople at this time."

Reply:

♦ "I can appreciate how you *feel*."

♦ "A lot of people I've spoken with *felt* that their bosses were too busy to see me."

♦ "But when they *found* out how much time they saved by using our product (or service), they were amazed. We'd like to see if there's an opportunity to do the same for you. Would Thursday be a good time to see him, or is next week better for him?"

Speaking With the Decision-Maker

There are times when you are able to bypass the gate-keeper and get through to the decision-maker directly. You may get some of the same objections you would get from the gatekeeper, and you can handle them in much the same way.

✦ **Consider using Feel, Felt, Found.** One of the most common objections you'll hear is "Business is slow right now; we're not making any purchasing decisions." You can use the three F's to reply:

> Quick Presentation Tip:
>
> If you're not enthusiastic about your product or service or don't believe there's value in what you're selling, you might as well get out of the business.

  ✧ "I understand how you *feel*."

  ✧ "Many of my present customers *felt* the same way."

  ✧ "But when they *found* out how our product (or service) helped them grow their business, by

61

getting them into new markets, they were amazed. I'd like to share some of their stories with you and see if we can do the same for you. Is Thursday morning good for you, or is the afternoon better?"

✦ **The "I don't have time to see you" objection.** Sometimes you have to go a step beyond Feel, Felt, Found. If the decision-maker consistently tells you that she doesn't have time to fit you into her schedule, say, "I'll tell you what. Share just 10 minutes of your time, and if I can't show you something of tremendous value to your company, I'll never call you again." Most of the time, the decision-maker will take you up on your proposal. Once you get into the meeting—if you've done your homework and know your value—your 10 minutes will expand into a full-blown presentation.

✦ **When all else has failed, make a last-ditch effort.** There are some situations when you've tried everything within your power and still make no connection. After you've made many attempts to get an appointment, there is one last-ditch tool you might want to try. A sales rep I know has used it, and says that 90 percent of the time, people will reply. So when you've tried everything else, try this fax:

May 1, 2005

[Name]
[Company]
Fax#:

Dear [Name],

I'm sure you have an excellent reason for not returning any of my calls.

Becuase I don't want to be a nuisance, please choose from the following options and fax this back to me at (123) 555-1234.

❏ I'm on safari and haven't gotten my messages.
❏ I've been drowning in work. Call me next week…I will take your call then.
❏ I am not working here anymore; call in care of NASA.
❏ I am sorry and will call you back soon.
❏ Please call me back at ____a.m./____p.m. on __/__/05
❏ I hate you and don't ever want to talk to you.
❏ Other _____.

Sincerely,

[Your name]

✦ **And if that doesn't work....** After you've tried faxes, phone calls, e-mails, and follow-up materials, after you've done everything else you can think of, if you're still not getting any response from the prospect, you might try leaving this message: "Every night before I go to sleep, I speak to God. Why can't I talk to you?" Believe it or not, this message has worked time and time again!

These examples may be going to an extreme, but it may also be the way you will finally get the appointment you seek. Sometimes, it takes a lot of time, effort, and creativity to get that appointment. Customers who appreciate that you have their best interests at heart will actually appreciate your persistence in getting in the door.

It's true that times are hard for many businesses. But that's always going to be true. Individual companies and industries go through prosperity cycles, just as the country's overall economy does. In good times and in bad, there will always be someone who says, "I just can't afford your product right now," or "The economy is taking a toll on our business and we've got to tighten our belts."

Ever since money was invented, people have been looking for bargains. Sometimes it's for purely economic reasons: "We have only a limited amount to spend and though we want your product, we can only pay so much for it." Sometimes it's for emotional reasons: "We want to be sure that we get what we pay for." Price objections arise, therefore, for two reasons:

1. The customer wants to get the best price possible.
2. The true value of what you're selling has not been conveyed to the customer.

BARRY FARBER'S GUIDE TO HANDLING SALES OBJECTIONS

When it comes right down to it, price is hardly ever the sole deciding factor in a sale. Think about it. When you're looking to buy a particular item, there are dozens of hot buttons that can get you beyond its price. Perhaps you *must have* the product right now (if you run out of printer toner just before a vital report is due, you'll pay for a new cartridge no matter what the price). Maybe it's something you've been searching out for months and haven't been able to find anywhere else. Or perhaps it is the salesperson who makes the difference, someone who convinces you that the value you'll be receiving will far outweigh the initial investment you make.

Getting Past Price Concerns

If you focus solely on price when selling your product or service, so will your customer. Are there ever sales that are made on price alone? Of course there are. Sometimes a good deal is a good deal (especially if it's a one-time purchase) and the person offering the lowest price will get the sale. Is price ever not a concern? Occasionally. Once in a great while, a customer might say, "Money is no object." But that's not the way most businesses are run. Everyone's concerned with money, so you've got to make sure your customers know what they're getting for the dollars they're spending.

✦ **Sell your true value.** Your main goal, as a salesperson, is to help the customer understand the true value of what you're selling. The best way to do that is for you to understand exactly how your product or service will benefit that customer. You need to understand how you can help that customer make money (not just how making the sale will be

> Quick Selling-Philosophy Tip:
>
> **You can't just sell to; you have to help sell through.** Keep this question in mind: How can you help your customer sell his product or service to *his* customer? Show your customers ways they can be creative in marketing your product to their customers. Focus on ways you can help them get more business, so they can buy more of your product beyond the initial purchase. Your customers will know that they're not just buying a product, they're buying someone who can help them build their company.

profitable for you or your company). The more you can show your customers how your product will help them grow or expand their business, or help make their business run more efficiently, the more likely they'll want to invest in what you're selling.

+ **Focus on the customer's needs.** This is the only way you can know how to sell your value to a customer. The more information you can get before you see the customer, or while you're on the sales call, the better chance you have of getting beyond the issue of price. The way to focus in on meeting the customer's needs is to ask questions like "What's your greatest challenge today?" If you know the greatest challenge facing that individual, you can start thinking about how your product or service might provide a solution to that challenge. The closer you can come to meeting that challenge, the easier it will be for them to see your product or service for what it *does* and not for what it *costs*.

Here's an example of how that works. I was making a sales presentation to five top company executives. They were expecting me to come in and "pitch" my product. Instead, as the meeting began, I said, "Before we talk about my product, I was wondering if I could ask each one of you a question. What is the greatest challenge you have today selling your product line?"

I got five different answers. While each person was talking, I took notes, and when they were all through, I said, "I appreciate those valuable insights into understanding your business and what you're going through. Here's how my product can help with each of those challenges...." This process told them that I was interested in their needs and concerns, and helped me understand how to present my product in the most positive light for this company. My presentation could then focus more on

> Quick Problem-Solving Tip:
>
> **Product knowledge = problem solving.** The more you know about your product and your company as a service provider, the more solutions you will have for your customers. The more solutions you can offer, the better you can offset any price objections that may arise.

solutions and less on price. If the product can solve the customers' problems, they'll pay a little more for it.

+ **Addition, subtraction, multiplication, division.** If you get a price objection, break it down into mathematical functions:

   ✧ Add up all the features and benefits your product or service offers.

   ✧ Subtract the features or services the customer won't get by going with the competition.

   ✧ Multiply by intangibles, such as service (you can deliver a quick turnaround, you're available by pager 24/7, and so on).

69

⋄ Divide by reducing to the ridiculous. Take your investment for the year and divide that number by 12 for the monthly cost. Divide that number by 30 to get the cost of "just pennies a day" for all the benefits and services you are offering.

✦ Separate yourself from the competition.

Objection example:

⋄ "I like your product, but I've seen it elsewhere for less."

Reply:

⋄ "I understand. What you want to know is if you're paying more for our product, what other value are you getting for that investment? Let me tell why our product is different from others like it on the market today...."

If price comes up too early, you can qualify budget, but don't forget to qualify your product or service beyond the price itself, to show where your unique value comes into the picture. When you say, "What you want to know is if you're paying more for our product, what other value are you getting for that investment?" customers will probably say something such as, "That's right." Then you're in a positive position to respond with content that comes after understanding your customer's situation. What makes you unique and stand out in a positive way? Why would a customer do business with you over somebody else? You have to differentiate yourself to the customer with at least three key things: "Here are three things that make us unique...." Stating an objection or saying no is comfortable for the customer; there's not much risk involved. To get past that no, find a new approach. Help him feel safe to make a positive decision by demonstrating why your solutions are unique and are the best for his business goals.

Quick Tip on Testimonials:

Testimonials are one way to sell your price against the competition's. There are times when customers go with lower-priced competitors. Often, they end up returning to you because the competitors' products or service were not satisfactory. When that happens, ask them for testimonials (written or tape-recorded), stating why they went with the competition, what happened when they did, and why they came back to you. You can then use the Feel, Felt, Found technique: "I understand how you *feel*. A lot of my customers *felt* the same way you do. But I want you to hear what they *found* when they went with a competitor for the lower price, and exactly why they came back for our product and service. Here's what they had to say...."

71

✦ **Price versus cost.** Help your customer understand the difference between price and cost. Price is the dollar amount you initially pay for a product or service, and cost is the customer's return on investment—what the investment will be for the life of the product or service and how much he will benefit from or save over time by using that product or service.

Objection example:

◇ "I can't afford to pay this much for your service."

Reply:

◇ "You know Mr. Smith, many years ago our company made a basic decision. We decided that it would much easier to explain price one time than it would be to apologize again and again for poor quality or service. (Pause.) And I bet you're glad we made that decision. It's impossible to pay a little and get a lot; a low price comes with some kind of sacrifice. And that sacrifice can cost you a lot in the long run."

Think in terms of investment, rather than expense. You must answer this question for your customers:

"How is this product (or service) an investment in the future of my business, rather than an expense with no return?" Let them know how your product or service can save them money in the long run, increase productivity, or bring them more customers. Let them know what you've learned about their com-

> Quick Price vs. Cost Tip:
>
> 1. Price.
> 2. Quality.
> 3. Service.
>
> *Please pick two.*
>
> (Sign seen in a copy shop.)

pany and how your product or service can enhance their business. Help them understand how spending money now will pay them future dividends.

◆ **Strengthen your relationships.** This is probably the most important factor of all in handling price objections. If the relationship is strong, it should win out over price every time because of the comfort level the customers feel with you. If they trust you, if they know that you are looking out for their needs and concerns, price becomes less of an issue. It doesn't matter whether you keep up your relationships by calling on customers every week, sending out monthly e-mails, or by sending handwritten notes once a quarter. What matters is that your goal is to find those customers who will benefit the most from what you have to offer, and then to form strong, solid relationships with those people.

✦ **Earn the sale.** The "replies" in this chapter are based on the assumption that you have earned the sale—that you have done the homework on the customers, that you have listened carefully, asked questions, found out what's important to them, and qualified them to be sure they actually can afford to pay for your product or service. No amount of "handling" will overcome a price objection if the money is simply not there.

In the long run, your goal is to sell customers on the many benefits that they'll receive over the life of the product or service they're buying. Once they understand that, it makes the decision a little easier—to invest a little more for the long haul. As British essayist John Ruskin once wrote:

"It is unwise to pay too much, but it is worse to pay too little. When you pay too much, you lose a little money—that is all. When you pay too little, you sometimes lose everything because the thing you bought was incapable of doing the thing it was bought to do. The common law of business balance prohibits paying a little and getting a lot—it cannot be done. If you deal with the lowest bidder, it is well to add something for the risk you run, and if you do that you will have enough to pay for something better."

If it weren't for objections, there would be no need for salespeople at all. You could just send out a brochure that listed all the features of a product, how much it cost, and that would be that. A customer would either buy from that brochure, or find another one that he liked better.

Luckily, for those of us who love sales, the world doesn't work that way. People will always have objections. And when you get right down to it, there are only two basic questions that people are always asking (no matter what they actually say): "What is this product or service going to do for me?" and "Why should I buy it from you?"

Those questions come out in various forms, including objections about:

+ Time.
+ Experience.
+ Credentials.
+ Need.

The reason I've put all these different types of objections into one chapter is because there's not often that much difference between how you handle different objections. What you say varies, of course, according to the issue you're addressing, but the concepts behind how you handle each of these objections remain the same. You use the same six-step method revealed in Chapter 2; you use Feel, Felt, Found (or your variation on it); you use questions to understand your customer's needs, goals, and concerns; and you look for solutions that will not only help solve the customer's immediate problem, but will cement your relationship for future sales.

In my career as a speaker and sales trainer, I've spoken to salespeople in every industry imaginable, including advertising, banking, communications, coffee, copiers, electronics, hospitality, publishing, real estate, and many more. When I ask them about the kinds of objections they hear, they all tell me the same ones, which tells me that the way you handle an objection remains the same from industry to industry. Objections are universal requests for more information. The objections I've included here are some of the most common ones salespeople across the United States tell me they hear every day. Use the objections and replies I've included here as examples, not as scripts. Adapt them to your product or service, your company, your industry, and most of all, to your individual style and personality.

Time Objections

Why do time objections arise? It's simple: People are busy. They want to get off the phone, end the meeting, or get back to the work they see as a more important way to spend their time. If you're making a sales call, especially if it's a cold call on the phone, you have no idea what's going on at the other end of the line. It could be that the customer is overwhelmed with work, or is on a tight deadline and truly does not have time to talk. Or it could be a stalling tactic, just to get you off the phone for the moment. The key is to explain why the time they invest in speaking with you is worthwhile, because it will either save them time in the long run or make them money down the line.

There are several ways to handle time objections:

Objection example:

    ❖ "I don't have time to speak with you right now."

Reply Option 1:

    ❖ The simplest, and sometimes best reply to that is often, "I can appreciate that your time is valuable. When would be a good time for me to call again?"

Reply Option 2:

✧ "That's exactly why I'm calling you. Our program actually helps people save time, and I'd like to see if we can do the same for you...."

Reply Option 3:

✧ "I understand that you're busy right now. Can you just answer one question for me now? What is the greatest challenge facing you and your company right now? Once you tell me the answer, I'll take some time to think about ways that my product can help you meet that challenge and call you back next week. Is Wednesday afternoon good for you? Or would Thursday morning be better?"

Objection example:

✧ "It's not the right time."

Reply:

✧ "I can appreciate that. A lot of my customers felt the same way. But when they saw the advantages that we provided them, they said it was the best time to see me. I'd like to see if we can do the same for you."

People say that timing is everything—but it's not the only thing. If the customer can't speak with you today, or even in the near future, that's no reason to give up. Ask if it would be all right to stay in touch. Learn as much as you can about the customer, and then send information that can gradually educate him on how he can benefit from your product or service.

> Quick Time-Objection Tip:
>
> Don't give up just because a customer says he can't see you now. Be persistent about calling back. But only call when you have something new to say, something that you know this customer would be interested in hearing and that would help the customer reach his goals. Then, when the time is right, the customer will say, "Let's get in touch with the salesperson who's been sending me all that information."

Objection example:

✧ "We need it sooner."

Reply Option 1:

✧ "How soon do you need it? And how important is it that you get it by that date?" (You want to find out if this is a real objection or if this is just a stall. You don't want to run around in circles trying to get an early delivery date if a later one will do.)

Reply Option 2:

❖ "Let me go back and check with my production department and see if we can have it to you by that date. I don't want to make a promise to you I wouldn't be able to keep—we don't do that with our customers." (You may lose out on this particular sale if you can't make the delivery date, but the customer will appreciate your honesty and probably buy from you in the future.)

Experience Objections

Why do experience objections arise? If customers have purchased products or service from you or company in the past, and they were satisfied, they'll probably want to buy from you again. Of course, the opposite is true as well. If they have had bad experiences with your products or company— or know someone else who had a bad experience—you'll have to work a lot harder to overcome their objections. You have to let them know how things have changed for the better—

what you are doing now that was not done before, how your technology has changed, how your company has been restructured—in other words, whatever will assure them they will have a better experience this time than they had before.

Objection example:

✧ "We used your product or service before and we didn't like it."

Reply:

✧ "Can you explain to me exactly what it was you didn't like about our product?" (Go back to the fundamentals of the six-step method and have them define the objection for you. Perhaps the problem they had with your product has been fixed in a later version. Perhaps they were not using it correctly. Once you know exactly what it was they didn't like, you can explain how things are different now.)

Objection example:

✧ "We know others who have used your product or service before and they didn't like it."

Reply:

⋄ "Do you know exactly what it was they didn't like about our product?" (This is practically the same as the previous objection. The customers may not be able to be as specific about the problem, but you can get the general idea.)

Objection example:

⋄ "We used a similar product or service before and we didn't like it."

Reply:

⋄ "Can you explain to me exactly what it was you didn't like about that product?" (This should be an easier objection to handle because once you know what the problem was, you can point out the differences between your product or service and the one they used before.)

Testimonials: The Power of a Second Opinion

When you come across experience objections (or credential objections such as the ones in the next section), the best way to handle them is to bring in a testimonial from one of your customers. Have you ever watched one of the home shopping networks on television or seen an infomercial? Then you know about the power of testimonials. I know, from my own experience selling products on QVC, that as soon as there's a phone call from a satisfied customer, there's an instantaneous increase in the number of sales. When real customers are seen or heard testifying as to how beneficial this product has been for them, potential customers are more likely to buy. It helps the prospect clearly imagine him- or herself already the proud owner of that product, experiencing the same benefits as the customer who made the testimonial.

The best way to get prospective clients to buy from you is to introduce them to other satisfied customers. Because it's not very practical to drag satisfied customers around with you on all your sales calls, testimonials can take their place. Luckily, you don't have to be on a shopping network or infomercial to use testimonials to your advantage.

Ask your best customers if you can "interview" them about the positive experiences they've had with your product and company, and record it on a video or digital camera. You can then load the videos onto your laptop computer, and play them back for prospective customers with just the click of a mouse.

For example, there are some instances when customers say that they know of others who have used your product or service and didn't like it. You can counter that statement by saying, "I understand that's what you heard from Mr. Jones. But I'd like to let you see for yourself what Mr. Smith had to say after he tried someone else's product, and then came to us for his next purchase."

This is the perfect customer to give you a testimonial. Then you can say to your reluctant prospects, "Here are some comments from a customer who had the same concerns as you do now. She chose competitor's product, but then came to us because of our higher quality and service. Here's what she had to say." You can then open your laptop and play the testimonial for your prospect immediately.

Ask your customers to talk about the benefits they've received from using your product or service. If you have many different testimonials, you can use the one that fits best into the sales scenario in which you find yourself. One rep I know takes pictures of customers using his product. A picture of a happy, satisfied customer is worth a thousand impersonal sales brochures. You can't get closer to the truth than when it comes from someone who has real life experience with you, your product, and your company.

Credential Objections

Why do credential objections arise? This type of objection only comes up when a customer is not familiar with you, your product, and/or your company. Let's face it, here you are, a stranger, trying to get this customer to put his trust in you and to part with his hard-earned money for something with which he is completely unfamiliar! That's a tall order. It's no wonder the customer has doubts. This may be a time, depending on what it is you're selling, when a free sample or trial period is in order, or a 30-day money-back guarantee. The idea is that once you get the customer to give your product or service a try, she'll like it so much she'll want to come back for more.

Objection example:

❖ "I've never heard of your product or service before," or, "I've never heard of your company before."

Reply:

❖ "I can appreciate that. We are new on the market. Some of our other customers had the same concerns. But after using our product, they found that what we had to offer was even more beneficial than the better-known product they had used in the past. I'd like to show you how we can do the same for you. (This is a perfect time to let your customer know what makes your product different from similar products out on the market. It's also the perfect time to use a testimonial from a satisfied customer.)

Objection example:

⋄ "We've heard negative things about your product (or service)."

Reply:

⋄ "Can I ask what it was you heard and who you heard it from?" (Once again, you want to get the customer to define the objection as specifically as possible. It may be that your competition is putting you down, or there may be a bad buzz going around the industry that you want to be aware of. You need to do a little digging so that you can provide the customer with the information he needs to make his own decision about your product or service.)

Need Objections

Why do need objections arise? In theory, a need objection will never come up because you've qualified your prospects so carefully. In reality, need objections come up during the qualification process. It's while you're introducing yourself, who you are, and what your product is about, that a customer will interrupt and say, "I don't need that," or "I already have someone who does that for us." These are the times when you have to stop and answer those objections before you move any farther ahead with sale.

Objection example:

⬧ "I have no need for your product (or service)."

Reply:

⬧ "I can understand where you're coming from, but maybe you can answer a few questions for me. I visited your Website and went to your downtown store, and I think that my service can help you out. Can you tell me a little bit about your goals and challenges so I can be sure my service really does fit your needs?" (By saying that you visited the Website and/or the store, you let the customer know that you've done your homework, and that you've already thought about ways you can be of benefit to him. The customer will probably be impressed that you already know so much about his business.)

Quick Tip on Need Objections:

Be relentless. Five years ago, I approached a decision-maker about doing sales training for his organization. He looked me in the eye and said, "We do not hire outside trainers." Plain and simple, no run around. I thanked him for not stringing me along, but told him, "I'm going to learn as much as I can about your company and your challenges, and one day I feel there's going to be an opportunity for us to work together." I spoke to him every few weeks for five years, calling with suggestions or ideas relating to his needs and concerns. Over time, we developed a strong relationship. Recently, he called to say that he was impressed with the way I'd been marketing a new product. He wanted to hire me to address his people on how to think out of the box and develop new markets. I was relentless in pursuing this account—not by constantly calling to say "Are you ready to buy?" but by building a relationship that I knew would pay off over time.

Objection example:

✧ "We don't use outside vendors."

Reply:

❖ You would start off by asking, "Why is that?" The customer might reply with something such as, "We've used them in the past and found they weren't as effective as our own internal resources." You would follow that by asking, "Can you expand on the problem you had in the past?" You want to get as much knowledge as you can about what caused them to stop using outside vendors. Then you can go back the Feel, Felt, Found scenario: "I had a customer you're welcome to talk to who felt the same way. But after she gave our service a try, she found that what we did was far beyond what she had experienced in the past. We ended up saving them her time and money, as it allowed the internal people at her company to concentrate on doing what they do best. I'd like to share how we can do the same for you."

Objection example:

❖ "You only offer the B product line and we also need the D product line."

Reply Option 1:

✧ "How important is the D line to you?" In certain situations—and if the prospective sale is big enough—you may want to explore ways to bring in the other line for this customer. But you don't want to invest thousands of dollars just to bring in one line for him if it's not something he really needs or is not of major importance to him. Here again, you have to ask questions so that you have enough knowledge about the company to be able to say, "Based upon what you told me about what you're trying to accomplish, it seems that having the service we provide would benefit more than having the D line because...."

Reply Option 2:

✧ "It is true that we can't supply you with D, but what makes us unique is that we've been specializing in manufacturing and distributing B for 20 years...." In this case, you would sell the value of the high quality you are able to maintain in B because it's the only thing you do (as opposed to trying to be all things to all people). So you might suggest that this customer buys the B line

from you, and gets the D products from someone else.

Reply Option 3:

✧ "We can't supply you with D, but I can suggest
someone who can." You can't meet the customer's
needs in every case. Sometimes the best thing you
can say is, "Based upon what you're looking for,
I don't think what we have right now is the best
answer to your problem. There is a company that
does offer a D product that seems to really fit
what you're trying to do right now." Obviously,
you don't want to recommend your competitor
all the time. But when that is indeed the best
solution for the customer, it makes sense. What
the customer sees is that you are selling in his or
her best interest. That means that when this customer needs a product or a service you *do* provide, you'll be the one who gets called on first.

CAUTION: Never knock the competition. If a customer
says, "XYZ company can do this for us and you can't," say,
"XYZ is a fine company. But let me tell you what makes us
unique and different." Go into the strengths of your product
that offset the weaknesses of the competition. "We're the

only company that can make deliveries to every single one of your locations within a 24-hour time period." When you say you're the only company, you're really pointing out the competitor's weakness without directly putting them down.

Objection example:

❖ "We already have a supplier for your type of product or service."

Reply Option 1:

❖ "That's exactly why I'd like to speak with you. Some of our customers use both our services and the competitor's because we offer different things, but some of them have switched totally to us and here's why...."

Reply Option 2:

❖ "Did you use a different supplier before you had the one you use now? What was the reason you switched to the company you're currently using?" While the customer is exploring those reasons, you may come up with a reason he should switch again, because your company can meet his needs even better than the company he's using now.

Five Ways to Differentiate Yourself From the Competition

In order to woo a customer away from a competitor, you have to ask yourself these questions: What can I offer that's different from my competitor? What can I offer to bring more business to my customer's business? What value does my product or service have that can add value to the customer's business?

Here are five proven ways to differentiate yourself from the competition:

1. **Superior Service.** Service is what keeps you in business for the long haul. It's your track record that builds your current customers' confidence in you, and attracts prospects to you. You've got to be able to say, "Try us, and we'll prove that we will consistently do what no one else will."

   Differentiation comes through outrageous service, and that outrageous service adds value in the eyes of the customer.

2. **Unique Value.** The best way to bring extra value to your customers is to understand their businesses better than anyone else out there. Get to know the companies, the people involved, and the industry

as a whole. It's your knowledge that will be the differentiating factor. When I do seminars, for example, I don't just do a needs analysis with the people who hire me. I spend many hours on the phone, not just with their salespeople, but with my customers' customers as well. I interview their customers on tape and play back some of the comments during the seminar. These customers tell the salespeople what they're doing right and what they're not doing that the customers would appreciate. This is something different that makes me unique and gives more value to my seminar.

The concept of adding value applies no matter what you sell. Every time you go into an organization and ask questions about the company's needs and goals, you have another opportunity to look for ways you can support their vision. A value-added approach to selling puts you in a whole new light for your customers. You become one of their company's assets, one that they will not trade in easily for another vendor.

3. **Customization.** When I get information from my customer's customer, it allows me to tailor my program directly to my customer's needs and concerns.

That's what every customer is seeking. Even though your product or service may be similar to others on the market, it's your job to make it as customer-specific as possible. The best companies have their R and D people calling customers constantly to find out how they're using their products, what they like about them, what they don't like, what would they change, and how they would make them easier to use. Old products are then modified and new products are designed to match the information gleaned from these customers. No matter what you sell—whether it's a product or a service—your differentiating factor should evolve from the knowledge and input you get from your end users.

4. **Selling Through.** In business to business, your real job is to be a sales rep for your customers. Your objective is to help them sell more of whatever they sell. The more you help your customers sell, the more they're going to order from you. You *sell through* by showing your customers how your product can provide solutions to their challenges. You can also help them sell by "bridging," connecting XYZ company with ABC company—even if you have no stake in pairing the two. For instance, if

I'm selling a product to the XYZ Advertising Spe-
cialty Company, I might refer them to ABC company (an organization I know uses advertising
specialties) even if my product is not involved. But
just by introducing the two companies, I become a
valuable—and differentiated—asset to both.

5. **Building Solid Relationships.** Striving for the previous four factors will definitely help you rise above
the product parity that is so prevalent today. But the
most important differentiating factor of all is who
you are and how you connect with your customers.
That's what makes you unique. How many times
have you heard of a salesperson leaving one company to join another and having all his customers
go with him? That's because each one of those customers had a special bond with that salesperson
that was stronger than the bond to the particular
product he sold.

If you want to impress potential customers, load up with
ammunition that separates you from your competitors. You
don't need to spend money on color and flash for your presentations or perform outrageous stunts to get noticed. You
do need to have two or three major points that demonstrate
your unique value, and you need to do your homework so

that your information is heavily focused on their goals and challenges. Stick to the basics. If you want to stand head and shoulders above the crowd, just remember to start from a solid foundation of service, value, and strong relationships.

If you want to know how to be a successful salesperson, there is one person who knows better than anyone else: your customer. Treat a customer well and you'll end up with a loyal buyer. But treat a customer badly and you'll run into more objections than you could ever imagine.

As I've said before, everyone makes mistakes. And for the most part, customers are a pretty forgiving bunch. But that only goes so far. Customers find some mistakes so annoying that they get in the way of doing business. This chapter includes 10 of them.

Mistake Number 1: Not Being Organized

This is really common sense. No customer wants to sit there and wait while you look through all your papers for the one piece of information you were sure you brought with you but now can't seem to find anywhere. Some salespeople feel they can wing it—that they can go into a sales call "blind" and still be effective and persuasive. They think their charm will win the day. But charm only goes so far. If the customer sees that you're unprepared for a meeting, he won't have much faith that you will be prepared to take care of his account. You've lost any credibility you might have had.

Customers don't mind if you don't have a ready answer to a question they throw at you. They'd rather you be honest and tell them, "I don't know the answer to that. Let me go back to office and do some research, and I'll give you a call tomorrow." But they do mind if you waste their time by saying, "I have that information with me. Wait a minute, I think I left in the car. No, wait, it should be here in my briefcase. Didn't I give that to you already? No? Okay, I'll e-mail you the info later."

When you have all the information about your prospect collected and organized before your meeting, when you have done your homework, talked to people, studied your product line, and know it inside out—when you have everything in order—not only do you make a much better impression, your clarity of thinking is much better as well. Your direction, your purpose, and your focus is much stronger, so you exude confidence when you walk in the door.

Mistake Number 2: Talking Too Much

If you've read many books about sales, you might get the impression that all you're supposed to do is ask questions and listen to the answers. Obviously, you have to talk at some point—you do eventually have to answer a customer's objections, and to present your product's features and benefits and demonstrate how they meet the customer's needs. For instance, you might answer an objection about poor service performance in the past by saying, "I can appreciate that, but we now have a whole new strategy in place to deal with service issues, which I know are important to you. Here's how it works...."

Customers get annoyed, however, when you just talk about your product without knowing what it is about your product or service that might be important to them. If you are prone to talking too much, try this in your next meeting. Sit back, and as the customer is talking, pull out a notepad and start taking notes. Listen to what the customer is saying, and how she's saying it. Tune in to what she's saying. Have the customer talk about what's important to her. Throw questions back to her: "Cheryl, you mentioned this is something you tried in the past with your company. Can you go into that a little more?" Or, "I heard you just introduced a new line. How's that going? What's your biggest challenge in getting that out on the market?" Be aware of how much you're talking before you've gathered all the information you need. If you're doing all the talking, that means you're not listening or learning. The customer will feel— and rightly so—that you're more interested in making the sale than in helping her find a solution. When you find you're talking too much, ask a question, sit back, and listen.

Mistake Number 3: Interrupting

Sometimes when a customer voices his concern, you can't help but get excited about the fact that your product or service can provide what you see as the perfect solution, and you want to let the customer know about it. So you interrupt and jump right in even before the customer has finished speaking. This is not only rude, it's dangerous. The customer will, of course, be annoyed that he was not allowed to finish his thought. What if the end of his thought had been, "…and that's why I want to place an order from you," and you cut him off before he could get there? More likely, as we discussed in the six-step method, you'll bring in a whole new objection the customer had never even considered. Let the customer finish speaking. Take a deep breath and take in what he's just said. Think about a response that makes sense. A pause is not only a courtesy to customers because it lets them speak their minds, but it also gives you time to prepare the right comeback, the right question, or the right solution for them.

Mistake Number 4: Lacking Sincerity

Sincerity comes from embracing and believing in what you are doing. When you are sincere, you are not false, hypocritical, or deceitful. Customers look for these qualities in salespeople, as well as earnestness, truth, candor, and frankness. They want to do business with people who are real, genuine, honest, straightforward, and trustworthy. When you believe in what you're doing, and you're truly there to serve the customer's best interest, you don't have to try to be sincere. You don't have to try to be excited. It comes out naturally. If you're not really sincere about what you're selling, you'd probably be better off doing something else. You can have all the skills and steps in this book working for you, but if a customer senses you're not sincere, that will come through louder than any words you can say. When

> "To give real service you must add something which cannot be bought or measured with money, and that is sincerity and integrity.
>
> —Douglas Adams, English novelist"

you are sincere, however, your true self comes through and you allow the customer to connect with you the person, not the salesperson.

Mistake Number 5: Not Analyzing Needs

When you're asking questions and you're really listening, you're learning things that are going to help you solve your customer's problems. If you are not asking questions and establishing need, you're doing nothing but presenting another gadget that's going to give the customer a headache. It takes an effective needs analysis to come up with solutions that overshadow the objections that concern your customers.

The top half of the illustration on the following page represents a sale that is lacking in needs analysis; the bottom half represents a sale with the proper ratio of needs analysis to presentation to close.

The top half of the illustration represents many beginning sales calls: The salesperson goes in, talks too much about his product or service, doesn't ask many questions, then makes a presentation that includes everything he ever learned about his product, whether it's appropriate to this customer or not. It's the old, "throw it against the wall and see what sticks" theory of selling. That leaves a large space at bottom layer of this pyramid for all the customer's objections.

The bottom half of the illustration is like an iceberg; the real strength lies beneath the surface. The needs analysis box is the largest, with the most room for asking questions: "Tell me about your business. How did you get started? What are the three most critical things you're looking for when investing in this type of product? Can you prioritize them? What is your greatest challenge today?" Then the presentation is shorter and tighter and focused solely around the customer's concerns: "You had mentioned that this was a key thing for you...." or "Because of what you said, I thought you might like to know that we can do this too." The bottom "Close" box is the smallest box. You don't need all that room for objections, because you focused on the customer's key needs, presented to those, answered objections before they arose, and then closed easily.

```
          ┌─────────────────────────────┐
          │       Needs Analysis        │
          │    (Not many questions)     │
          └─────────────────────────────┘
      ┌─────────────────────────────────────┐
      │            Presentation             │
      │   (Scattered, not focused on needs) │
      └─────────────────────────────────────┘
   ┌───────────────────────────────────────────┐
   │                   Close                     │
   │            (Lots of objections)             │
   └───────────────────────────────────────────┘
   ─────────────────────────────────────────────
   ┌───────────────────────────────────────────┐
   │               Needs Analysis                │
   │            (Lots of questions)              │
   └───────────────────────────────────────────┘
      ┌─────────────────────────────────────┐
      │            Presentation             │
      │   (To the point; focused on needs)  │
      └─────────────────────────────────────┘
          ┌─────────────────────────────┐
          │            Close            │
          │      (Fewer objections)     │
          └─────────────────────────────┘
```

Mistake Number 6: Being Too Pushy

Customers often complain about salespeople who are too pushy and who try to "convince" them they need a product or service that doesn't fit their business or answer their needs. The truth is, you can't really convince anyone to purchase anything. What you *can* do is make it worthwhile for this customer to make a positive buying decision by demonstrating the value of what you're selling.

You're being pushy and aggressive when your only goal is to make a sale and the customer's concerns don't matter to you. You're being pushy when you make the customer feel wrong or guilty for stating her concerns or asking questions. You're being assertive when you believe 100 percent in your product or service and that what you're selling can be of benefit to this customer. You're being effective when you respect the customer's right to object.

There's often a fine line between being aggressive and being assertive. There's nothing wrong with pushing your idea. But when the customer sees that you're pushing solely for your own interest, when there's no understanding of the customer's point of view, that's when you'll get "stalling" objections: "I have to think about it," or "I have to consult my partner about this."

One of my partners is also one of the greatest sales-people I know. He is very soft spoken, he listens to customers, and he's always calm and low-key. Customers see him almost as a father figure. But he sells. When he says something, he says it with great authority: "Here's what we're going to do...." He has a quiet strength that customers respect. He also lets his customers know, even when they're voicing concerns, that he is totally on their side. Customers don't look to him as a salesman—they look to him for answers.

Mistake Number 7: Reciting a Script

We've all run into them at one time or another—the salesperson who gives you the sense that if you interrupt his pitch, you ruin his whole presentation. Maybe you're in a meeting with a salesperson and the phone rings. You take the call, and when you get back to the salesperson and say, "Sorry for the interruption. Go on," he begins at the beginning again or takes up exactly where he left off. The presentation sounds like something he's prepared verbatim. It's fine to prepare an outline of where you're going and what you're trying to accomplish. In fact, that's critical. When I talk with my partners about going into a meeting, for instance, we prepare beforehand what we're going to talk about, how we're going to present our ideas, what we will do in various scenarios. We do this in general terms. We don't know exactly what we're going to say, but we know we can rely on our overall knowledge and our specific preparation for this meeting.

The most successful salespeople are great on their feet. When they're thrown curve balls and objections in a meeting, they can handle them and get back on track. You don't want your training to show. It becomes a turnoff. You must treat each customer individually and have enough confidence in your knowledge and skills to know that you will be able to handle the situation without planning exactly what you're going to say.

Mistake Number 8: Not Building Rapport

Everybody wants to buy from someone he likes, trusts, and respects. Customers have to feel comfortable with you. This means that they find you agreeable to deal with and take pleasure in your company. You don't have to become best friends with every prospect or customer, but within the context of buyer/seller interactions, customers want to know that you are friendly, respectful, considerate, and accommodating. They trust you when they have confidence that you're there in their best interest (as well as your own—they know you're there to sell them something). This is a trust that you earn as you go, from your initial meeting through the closing of the sale, as well as through customer service and follow-through. They respect you when they see that you are an expert in your field with a thorough knowledge of their company and industry.

Customers want to see who you are. If you try to "act like a salesperson," customers will see right through you. They want to make a connection with you so that they can feel good about buying from you. If they don't trust you and don't feel comfortable with you, they will bring up more objections—and the objections will be harder to handle.

Mistake Number 9: Getting Defensive

If I told you that I've never gotten defensive in a sales call, I would by lying. When you believe in your product or service strongly and believe that it can truly benefit customers, it is only natural to get defensive if somebody questions that product or doesn't see the benefit. We want to defend what we believe in. However, when you get defensive, what you actually display is a lack of confidence. That's when you start feeling that you have to keep talking to try to convince and persuade and push that customer

> Belief is the knowledge that we can do something. It's the inner feeling that what we undertake, we can accomplish. For the most part, all of us have the ability to look at something and to know whether or not we can do it. So in belief, there is power: our eyes are opened; our opportunities become plain; our visions become realities.
>
> —Wynn Davis, author of *The Best of Success*

into seeing things your way. That never works. Perhaps there is information about the customer that you've missed. Perhaps the customer has misunderstood something you've said about your product or service. Perhaps you've tried to close before you've established rapport. Whatever the reason, when you get defensive, you end up arguing with the customer. When that happens, you have already lost. Instead, take a deep breath and ask questions about why the customer feels the way he does: "Can you go into more detail about your concerns?" That way, you can gain a better understanding of the customer's problem, and give yourself time to think about how you're going to come back with a proper explanation to settle his uneasiness.

Mistake Number 10: Taking It Personally

Let's face it. Salespeople, like entrepreneurs, actors, writers—in fact, most people—face rejection every day. Whatever you're doing in life, there are going to be some people who just don't like you, who disagree with you, or who don't think what you're doing or what you're selling is important. When you face that kind of rejection, there are three things you can do.

Your first choice is to ignore it, which is difficult

> A great attitude does much more than turn on the lights in our worlds; it seems to magically connect us to all sorts of serendipitous opportunities that were somehow absent before the change.
>
> —Earl Nightingale

at best. If you're good at sales, you take pride in what you do, you have confidence and enthusiasm, and you don't like being turned down.

The second kind of reaction is to let rejection motivate you. That's what I do. First, I look at where the rejection is coming from. Who is the "rejector"? How knowledgeable is he? How much does he know you as an individual and what you can do? I might even call him back to find out just what the problem is: "Can you help me understand exactly what is it that is stopping us from moving forward or what it is that's holding you back?" Maybe it's something I can fix or solve. At least it gives me an opportunity to solve it; doing nothing leaves me at a dead end. In that way, objections become a motivating factor and not an obstacle.

The worst way to deal with rejection is to let it get to you and start believing what the other person is saying. Successful salespeople know it's not the rejection that's important, it's what we do with it. Particular situations may get them down, but they will not let those situations take them out of the game. If they can't get to a difficult prospect today, they make a long-term plan to keep trying to make contact over the next six months or a year. If a great deal

> Sales are contingent upon the attitude of the salesman—not the attitude of the prospect.
>
> —W. Clement Stone, U.S. businessman and philanthropist

falls through, they study what went wrong and improve their approach for the next time. If they can't change a situation, they change their attitude about it. They don't let—they won't let—the world defeat them.

The world will never defeat you, if you have confidence in yourself and your abilities. In the next chapter, you'll learn that confidence is one of the strongest weapons you'll ever have against any obstacles that arise.

If you've ever watched an Olympic competition, you've seen the faces of champions reflect not only the hard work and preparation that's gone into that moment, but also the confidence they have going into the arena. That confidence is not just what carries them through, it's what communicates their position before the event even starts. They cannot win without this confidence. Their competitors can sense fear, insecurity, and unpreparedness, just as a customer can sense these things in a salesperson who doesn't feel confident. Once they sense a lack of confidence, it makes it easier for them to bring up objections, and more difficult to answer them.

Here are three things you can do to build, maintain, and project the confidence you need:

+ **Prepare.** When you walk into calls, you have to have done your homework, studied your customers' businesses, talked to their customers, read their annual reports, and know what problems they have before they're even aware of them.

117

To understand the importance of preparation, think about your days in school. Some people are not very successful students. They don't know how to study, or they don't understand the value of studying. Then, when test time rolls around, they dread taking the exam because they're so afraid of failure. Those who realize the value of doing homework and being prepared for every class and every exam are able to walk in to every test with confidence, knowing they have done as much as they possibly could to make this a positive experience.

> One important key to success is self-confidence. An important key to self-confidence is preparation.
>
> —Arthur Ashe,
> U.S. tennis player

That's the kind of confidence you need when you're walking into a sales call or meeting. Your success depends 99 percent on your attitude going in. If you're hesitant, customers will see right through that before you even pull out your notebook. If you're confident, based on the amount of preparation you've put in, you eliminate many of the objections customers would have had if they suspected a lack of knowledge on your part. And because you've done your homework, you'll be much more effective at handling the objections that do come up. You'll be calmer, because you know the answers. You can let the customer talk, then pause, relax, get your thoughts together, and answer based on everything you learned about them.

When I want to prepare to make a sales call, here's what I do: I go to the customer's Website and print out some of the materials I find there. I search the Internet for information and articles about the company to try and find out what the customer is doing successfully and where some of his weaknesses may lie. I also look for general information about the industry if it's one I haven't sold to before. If I can, I talk to other people who are involved in or knowledgeable about their industry and who might be able to give me insights about what's important to that kind of company. I write down some questions I would like to ask the customer and think about questions he might possibly have for me. By the time I get to the sales call, I'm confident that I'm as prepared as I can be for this sales call—no matter what objections I may encounter.

Another reason I am confident when I go into sales calls is because I visualize a successful outcome.

> The mind is the limit. As long as the mind can envision the fact that you can do something, you can do it—as long as you really believe it 100 percent.
>
> —Arnold Schwarzenegger, governor of California

One thing that great achievers have in common—no matter what their field or occupation—is the ability to visualize their goals and dreams. They have a clear, focused picture of their destination, and it is this clear picture that they strive toward, no matter what obstacles may appear before them. That doesn't mean they always reach their goals or that they turn out 100 percent the way they visualized them to be. But they never lose their ability to sustain a positive vision of the future, and the belief that their visions will pull them forward and make them strong.

That vision, plus your preparation, will allow you to fill your presentation with extra details customized to the customer's business. There's an old saying that goes, "Luck happens when preparation meets opportunity." When you walk into an account with that kind of excessive preparation, you exude a quiet confidence and strength in the way you walk, in your handshake, and in the way you look into somebody's eye. Sometimes, that's all you need to close the deal.

✦ **Immerse.** Bobby Fisher is one of the greatest chess players who ever lived. From the second he woke up until the second he went to sleep, all he thought about was chess. Admirers said he was able to get "underneath" the chessboard because of his passion for the game. People who have a passion for what they do and what they sell have a deep foundation of confidence that, in itself, breeds success. The highest achievers I know live, sleep, eat, and breathe their business. They're always thinking about opportunities and presenting them to other people. They're not obnoxious; they're pumped up, and their enthusiasm is contagious. To be successful in sales is to be so immersed in your business that you walk it and talk it and build your confidence every day. When you walk in the door with that state of mind, you close the deal before you even ask the question. Are you going to get objections? Of course. But there's nothing that keeps you grounded and allows you to handle curve balls like having that solid passion for what you sell and its value to your customer.

I have been in sales all my working life. I love selling, and at one point, when I was younger, I was a
"sales juggler," selling several different products at
once. I sold home improvement products over the
phone at night; on weekends I sold real estate; and
during the day I sold advertising for a start-up fashion
magazine. I was used to a fast pace and quick sales.

Then I took a full-time job selling office products.
The first year and a half was a difficult time for
me. The quick sales were gone. This was a service-
oriented business; the sales cycle could take anywhere from 30 days to several months before you
got an order. I was an average performer. I had my
good months and my not-so-good months. But I felt
something was missing. For the first time, I questioned
whether or not this was the right field for me.

Then one day I read an article that talked about a
technique I suggested in Chapter 5, in which you
interview satisfied customers on a tape recorder and
use these testimonials to show other prospects how
you might help them. I decided to try it—and it
turned my selling life around. My prospects were
impressed and I got totally pumped up hearing the
first-hand benefits my customers were receiving.

Once again, I became enthusiastic about selling, and my enthusiasm was catching. I had been selling two copiers a month; now I was selling 10. For a year and a half, I couldn't get into the business—and then the business got into me. I resuscitated my passion for sales by finding a unique and creative way to differentiate myself from the competition, which put my energy and enthusiasm back on track.

So what do I do if I ever feel myself getting off track again, if I have a sales call scheduled and I'm not quite feeling up to par? I think about how important each and every sales call is, and how hard I have worked for what I have achieved so far. I keep my goals in front of me, and I'm always reaching for more. Write down your goals and keep them where you can see them—whether it's to exceed your sales quota, to be the best in your field, or to accomplish something that no one else in your company has ever done. That drive and that passion will be the engine that fuels your confidence.

✦ **Know where your value lies.** Another building block of confidence is the ability to articulate the reasons people should do business with you. What is it that differentiates you and your product or service from the competition? You should always be prepared with at least three factors that separate you from the crowd. Use your knowledge of the customer and your knowledge of your product and service to develop those three key factors, and they will enable you to make your presentation from a position of unassailable strength.

When it comes to selling, many words and phrases are tossed casually about. You've probably heard the phrase "value-added selling" dozens of times. But do you really know what it means? It means more than focusing on the value of your product and the service behind it, but also on the value that you personally bring to the sale.

Successful salespeople are not content to do what every other salesperson does for their customers. They go beyond. They are constantly asking themselves and their customers, "What else can I offer?"

If adding value for your customers is not a high priority for you, you will not be able to compete in today's marketplace. Every time you turn around, there is another product out on the market that is just like yours—exactly like yours. Where, then does your value lie?

It lies within you. You must be the final deciding factor that makes a prospect choose your product over all the others. Even if your prospect doesn't buy from you right away, let her know that, when you call again (or write or send an e-mail or any other communication), it will be to hook into her goals and challenges. You may even have an opportunity to introduce that customer to someone who can help her business—even if it has no immediate benefit for you. Your payoff will come later, when the customer needs your type of service and, because of your consistency in bringing added value, calls you for the business.

A value-added approach to selling puts you in a whole new light for your customers. You become one of their company's greatest assets, one that they will not trade in easily for another vendor or a lower price.

It all comes down to three of the most powerful words in the English language, "Yes I Can." Years ago, in one of his audio programs, Earl Nightingale told a story

> " If you have no confidence in self, you are twice defeated in the race of life. With confidence, you have won even before you have started.
>
> —Marcus Garvey, Jamaican political leader "

about a team of six American mountain climbers at the bottom of a mountain. A psychologist doing a survey asked each of them one question: "Can you make it to the top?" Five of the climbers answered with variations of, "I've been training for this for years. I'll make the best effort possible." One climber, however, answered simply, "Yes I can." Not only was he the first to the mountaintop, because of inclement weather, he was the only one.

There is something about the power of confidence that can move mountains; once we understand this in selling, 90 percent of all obstacles vanish before we even begin to climb.

Chapter 9
KNOWING WHEN TO WALK AWAY

Is it ever appropriate to answer an objection by saying, "You know what? I have to agree with you here. My product (or service) and your company are not a great match. Thanks for your time"? Salespeople are taught—in fact, they're drilled on the saying—"Never take no for an answer." Never give up. Keep trying until you find a way to get through. That's good advice—most of the time. But there *are* those times when it is appropriate for salespeople to walk away from potential business, times when no is the only appropriate answer.

Another basic business "truth" we've heard since the beginning of business is that the customer is always right. And, for the most part, that is also true. But there are times when it's appropriate to tell a particular buyer—the one who saps your strength and wastes your time again and again—that although the customer may be right, the relationship is wrong.

I'm not saying to get rid of every customer who is difficult to deal with. I'm suggesting that it may be time to weed out your customer base so that you can harvest the greatest rewards. Here are some ways to do that:

+ **Know when to walk away.** Persistence is a value-added quality in selling. But if you've tried again and again to reach a prospect who "doesn't get" your product or service, who doesn't see the value, or with whom you can't establish a connection, it may be time to walk away. If you're being stubbornly persistent about sticking to a path that doesn't lead anywhere, that's counter-productive; you want to spend your time where you're getting results.

  Some customers are simply rude and disrespectful. Others may be unrealistically demanding, wanting service that is impossible for you (or anyone else, for that matter) to provide. If this demanding customer is your only prospect, you may feel you have to stick it out. But when you have enough activity going on, you don't have to take business that it is going to produce more headaches than revenue.

  Some customers are just not worth the aggravation, for example those who are constantly asking you to do things for them, such as "throw in" extra parts or supplies for free or give them more of a discount. If the customer cannot see the value of your product or service, it's time for you to say no.

Leaving this kind of customer is not a failure; it only shows how much you value your time and product.

♦ **Follow the 80/20 rule.** Take stock of your customers. Who are the ones giving you most of your business? Who are the ones giving you most of the headaches? How much time are you spending with each? Of your total business, 80 percent comes from only 20 percent of your customers; focus on those customers that have the highest potential of increasing your bottom line. You must make a realistic evaluation of the cost of doing business with a high-maintenance customer. If someone demands constant attention and a huge amount of work for very little return, you won't be able to spend quality time with other customers who may be bringing in a higher profit.

♦ **Ask the difficult questions.** Too many salespeople are "stuck" with problem customers, because they don't ask the hard questions. They get sucked into a long, drawn-out sales process, because they have never asked, "Is there anyone else who is involved in making this decision?" They spend a lot of time with an indecisive customer because they haven't asked, "What's our next step?" or "What do we need to do to reach a decision by the end of this month?" They're afraid of rejection, afraid of objections. But getting an objection is often the only way to truly understand how the customer is thinking and get the sale back on track—or realize that this track is not the right one for you or your customer to follow.

Sell From the Top Down

Don't let yourself get in the position of selling to the wrong people because you are afraid of calling on the big guns. Don't assume they won't take your call. You'll probably have to keep trying, but they are the best resources you can find to give you a clear overview of the company's needs and concerns, and to direct you to the people who handle your type of product or service—vital information if you're selling to large companies with multitudes of divisions and confusing job titles. Even if you don't get to speak to the president or CEO, that person's assistant may be able to point you in the right direction. When the assistant says, "Bob Jones handles that," you can call Mr. Jones and say that you've just been speaking with the president's office and were told to speak with him.

♦ **Ask yourself some difficult questions.** For instance, "Am I presenting to the right person?" If the answer is no, it may not be possible at this point to go over his head and get to the decision-maker. Then ask yourself "Have I done everything I could? Do I understand the customer's needs? Have I presented a strong solution? What is it that's holding them back? Could it be that he just doesn't like me?" That is always a possibility. After all, try as we might, there are some customers with whom we just can't make a connection. That's when it's time to ask yourself, "Is it better to cut my losses now and move on the next account?"

Measure your return on investment (ROI). How do you know when it's time to end the relationship? First, you have to know what your value is. You have to have the confidence and belief in yourself and your product or service to be able to say, "I can spend this amount of time with this customer, and no more. I can sell my product or service for this price, and no less." Then, you have to take the time to do a thorough and honest ROI analysis. How many times have you called on this customer without moving the sale forward? Is the time you're putting into this account worth what you're getting back?

131

Leave the door open. Never lock the door behind you when you go. There's no point in telling a customer, "You're not worth my time." Say instead, "I appreciate the time you've invested with me, but it doesn't look like this is a good match for us." You might even recommend another product or service you think might fit his or her needs. Try to walk away on friendly terms so that both of you have the option to call again, if the situation should change.

The next time you deal with a difficult customer, ask yourself this question: "Is the time that I'm taking with this customer taking time away from others who need me more?" If the answer is yes, then it's time to cut your losses and walk away. If your first thought is to say, "the customer is always right," stop and ask yourself, "is this customer right for me?"

Chapter 10
ESSENTIAL ELEMENTS OF THE SALES CYCLE

In the simplest of terms, a sales cycle refers to a series of events that you go through with a customer, from the initial introduction to the close and follow-through. There are short sales cycles and long sales cycles, depending on (among other things) the type of product you're selling, the cost of the item, and who your customers are. There are innumerable variations on sales cycles, but they all have several elements in common.

The important thing to remember is that with every element of the sales cycle that is done correctly and effectively, you reduce the number of objections you're going to get by a wide margin. Objections arise when you're selling to the wrong market, when you're not asking the right questions, and when you're making presentations that aren't geared toward customers' needs. When you haven't met the standards that each of these steps requires, you'll never get beyond the objections to reach the close.

Following are the five most common elements of the sales cycle.

Prospecting

Prospecting is the art of looking for customers in all the right places. If you pick the wrong people to call on, you're going to have a much more difficult time selling your product. It's like a manager who hires the wrong person. No amount of training, coaching, and motivating will help mold someone who is not right for the job into the company's best employee.

How you prospect depends, once again, on what it is you're selling, whether your company gives you sales leads and a territory to mine or whether you're the one who determines where to look for customers. One of the products I market is geared toward children, so I want to sell to companies who sell to kids. One way I prospect is to go to stores that sell children's products, go to the racks, and check out the product packaging. When I find a product that I think is in a similar category to mine, I look on the back of the package and find the address, phone number, and/or Website of the company. Because these are companies that already have real estate in these stores, they are logical prospects to go after to see if they will carry my product.

Often, prospecting is seen as a numbers game—the more prospects you have, the greater your chances of making a sale. That is true, and the most successful salespeople, no matter what they're selling, live, sleep, and eat prospecting. But they also know that it's the quality of the time they spend prospecting that makes the difference; it's not just the numbers that count, it's how they can show qualified prospects the added value they bring. Here are four ways they do it:

1. **Cultivate the gatekeepers.** In Chapter 4, on appointment objections, we talked about getting past the gatekeeper. But sometimes the best way to storm the gate is to make friends with the gatekeeper. The decision-maker's assistant or secretary can be your greatest ally; he or she often has more influence than we give credit for. When an assistant has been helpful to me, I'll call the receptionist and get his or her full name and the address. Then I send a card that says, "Time. Your most valuable commodity" on the front, and on the inside, "Thanks for sharing some of it with me." I hand write a line or two inside, insert my business card, and mail it off immediately. It's amazing, the difference that small step makes the next time I call.

2. **Call potential prospects during off hours.** The worst
   time to try and reach decision-makers is during the
   day, when he or she is on the phone or running to
   meetings. Instead, call at 7:30 or 8 a.m., before everyone gets there, or at 5:30 or 6:00 when
   everyone's left. Call the Friday before holiday weekends when most people are in a good mood and the
   office is emptying out. Try Saturday mornings. Many
   high level executives go into the office when it's
   quiet and they can get paperwork done. They'll be
   more likely to speak to you if you're the only one
   calling. It also shows them that you're working as
   hard as they are, and will likely continue to do so
   after you sell them something.

3. **Cultivate creativity.** One of the most successful real
   estate agents I ever met got most of her business
   through a gas station. She made friends with the
   attendant at the station she patronized, and gave
   him her business card. This station was the first one
   off the highway into an area where many new homes
   were being built. She asked the attendant to give
   her card to anyone who stopped to ask for direc-
   tions or ask about a Realtor. She made many new
   contacts this way.

Remember this saying that I once found in a fortune cookie: Those who have a thing to sell and go and whisper in a well, aren't so apt to get the dollars as one who climbs a tree and hollers.

4. **Be tenacious.** Keep trying new ways to get the account. Send prospects new and updated information that might assist them in making their decision. Keep sending notes, faxing, and e-mailing ideas of value to them. Or send them a chocolate sneaker with a card that says, "Now that I got one foot in the door, I'd like to find ways we can help your organization with our products and services." When the time comes to buy, it is your name—and your tenacity—they will remember.

Great salespeople have many traits in common. They ask smart questions, know how to close, and have excellent follow-through.

> Nothing in the world can take the place of persistence. Talent will not; nothing is more common than unsuccessful men with talent. Genius will not; unrewarded genius is almost a proverb. Education will not; the world is full of educated derelicts. Persistence and determination alone are omnipotent.
>
> —Calvin Coolidge, former U.S. President

137

But the one trait they demonstrate more consistently than any other is constant prospecting, enhanced by creative approaches that build value and relationships.

To put it in other words, great salespeople see opportunity everywhere—and they make the calls. They know it's not *just* the numbers, but the numbers are what count.

Qualifying

Every question you ask is a qualifying question. There are, of course, basic questions that uncover needs, time frame, budget, and decision-makers. But all your questions should be designed to help you determine if your product or service is right for this prospect (and that's what qualifying is all about, isn't it?). Qualifying questions help you understand the uniqueness of each prospect. Take notes so that you can document key points and pick up what's most important to a prospect. Closing is not difficult when it is a natural extension of your relationship with a prospect, based upon your understanding of the benefits your product or service can provide him.

Asking the right questions is essential to making sure your product is a good match with each prospective customer. In other words, you've got to qualify that the person you're speaking to has a need for your product or service, has the money, and has the authority to buy. Otherwise, you end up wasting a lot of time—yours and the customer's.

Many beginning salespeople end up going back to a potential customer several times because they really don't understand which product the customer wants or needs. They have just one qualifying question: "Before we get started, if I could show you something that could benefit you and your business, do we have a basis for doing business today?" And they fully expect the prospect to say yes. What could he possibly object to in that question? But they don't really know where to go from there. They have no idea what would benefit that prospect; consequently, they have no way to move the sale forward.

Experience teaches that you have to ask questions to pinpoint each customer's needs and desires. If you don't qualify customers properly, you not only waste a lot of time, you ultimately hurt your reputation, and your company's as well.

Presentation

Sales calls come in as many different shapes and sizes as there are products to sell. Some sales calls are really just extended conversations, where both seller and buyer profit from the end result. For most salespeople, however, there comes a time when a more formal sales presentation is necessary to close the deal.

Here are five steps you can take in any situation to make your presentations powerful and persuasive:

1. **Prepare, prepare, prepare.** Before you make any presentation, you must complete a thorough needs analysis so that you uncover the prospect's hot buttons and address the prospect's needs. Make notes of the most important things you want to cover (don't, however, read from your notes directly—people get a much stronger message when it is spoken from the heart instead of the page). Do as much research as possible. Peter Conneley, currently President and CEO of Global Advertising and Marketing for *www.tommy.com* (a division of Tommy Hilfiger), says salespeople who come unprepared have no chance of doing business with him.

> "Whatever failures I have known, whatever errors I have committed, whatever follies I have witnessed in private and in public life have been the consequence of action without thought.
>
> —Bernard Baruch, statesman

"Sometimes people will come in with a presentation," he says, "and tell me they have a great idea for my company. But when I ask if they've seen any of our new stores, they say no. And when I ask if they've seen our new ad campaign, they say no.

If I were going to meet the head of marketing for a corporation, I would certainly review the ad campaign. If they haven't, that's the end of their presentations."

2. **Follow the four Ts.** Don't launch into your solutions immediately. Start with a short introduction. Build rapport with the people in the room. Make sure everyone is comfortable, and that you know how much time you have. Then follow the four Ts of presentations:

⋄ *Tell them what you're going to tell them.* Let them know what to expect in the presentation, and why your solution makes sense. For instance, you might say, "I'm now going to take you through our new product line and demonstrate exactly how it will help you decrease production time."

⋄ *Tell them.* Go through your presentation following the outline you just proposed.

⋄ *Test them.* Keep your prospect involved. Don't just spit out information; ask questions that will let you know if the presentation is hitting home and addressing his criteria. Ask "Is that important to you?" or "Do you see how this could

141

help eliminate the service problem you had in the past?"

✧ *Tell them what you told them.* Summarize your ideas and the most important benefits you covered in your presentation. Leave the prospect with the knowledge that you have hit on the points that are most important to him.

3. **Be yourself.** Don't worry about making your presentation perfect; concentrate on making your content strong and powerful. Speak as if you were having an informal one-to-one conversation, no matter how many people you're actually addressing. Once you've done your preparation and know the four Ts, you can relax and let your personality come through.

4. **Present with passion and pizzazz.** You don't have to be an entertainer or magician, but you do need enthusiasm and a positive attitude. A study conducted by Harvard Business School determined that four factors are critical to success in business: information, intelligence, skill, and attitude. When these factors were ranked in importance, this particular study found that information, intelligence and skill, combined, amounted to 7 percent of business success,

and attitude amounted to 93 percent! If you're not enthusiastic about your presentation, it doesn't matter how much you prepare or how many hot buttons you hit; you will lose your audience before you get anywhere near the close.

5. **Remember that technology is just a tool.** There's an old saying that goes, "If you can't convince them, confuse them." Some salespeople, intentionally or not, get so caught up in fancy graphic displays and overloaded slides, they forget about getting their core message across. If you need to use graphics and handouts, fine. Just don't let your audience miss your message because they're overwhelmed with technologically perfect, but meaningless, information.

Franklin Delano Roosevelt may have had the best advice ever for anyone giving a presentation: "Be brief. Be sincere. Be seated." Keep your presentation short, strong, and focused. Speak from the heart, get your message across—and be seated.

Closing

I've been in the business of sales my whole life. Every single day, I'm either selling something myself or training others to be better salespeople. I have studied every closing

143

technique ever put forward. Not only that, I've interviewed thousands of the top sales reps in the country, and they've also studied every closing technique, and come to the same conclusion. The bottom line is if you can't simply say to your customer, "Why don't we go ahead with this," there's something wrong. Not with your closing, but with your approach to sales.

The truth is that no one has yet discovered a closing technique that works unless it is built on a strong foundation.

If you want to know what the best closing techniques are, ask your customers. They'll tell you things such as: "The best sales reps come in here and know my business. They know who I sell to, they know what I need. They don't approach me with some generic presentation they learned by rote. They make me feel like I'm their first and best customer."

Every day you have to live with a sense of urgency: "I have a lot on my plate; how can I move things forward today?" But closing only has weight when it's backed by the steps you take before you ask for the order:

1. **Rapport.** If a customer doesn't like you, doesn't trust you, and doesn't feel comfortable with you, then it doesn't matter what closing technique you use.

You don't have to be friends with all your customers, but you do have to establish some kind of bond. And how do you do that? First, by getting to know that person, understanding his or her business, and discovering how your product or service can be of benefit. The second and most important method of establishing rapport is achieved by following the best advice ever given: Be yourself. It's the only way I know to make a meaningful connection with another person. If that connection doesn't happen (and there will be instances when it doesn't), then you may be better off not doing business with that individual.

2. **Relationships.** The objective of establishing rapport is to form a relationship. Some relationships are built quickly; others take time to blossom. Some are purely on a professional level, others are more personal. Part of building a relationship is being able to adapt to each customer's personality. I recently had a meeting with a potential customer in which we didn't even talk business for the first half hour. We chatted about his hobbies and interests. He needed that time to make a connection with me. Then we were able to proceed with the sale, and I closed by

asking, "Why don't we go ahead with this?" Of course, along the way, I asked simple questions like "Wouldn't you agree?" to get a series of "yes" responses. These small agreements, or trial closes, test the buyer and build towards the sale.

Relationships may take minutes to form, or they may take months; either way, it's the key to getting new customers and keeping old ones on board.

3. **Needs analysis.** I remember a story I once heard about a guest on *The Tonight Show* when Johnny Carson was the host. The guest was billed as the greatest salesman who ever lived. Johnny started off by saying, "You're the greatest salesman in the world—sell me something." Johnny expected his guest to go into a razzmatazz sales spiel. Instead, the man said, "What would like me to sell you?" "I don't know," Johnny replied. "How about this ashtray?"

"Why, Johnny?" asked the guest. "What is it that you like about that ashtray?" Carson began to list the things he liked: the fact that it matched the brown color of his desk, that it was octagonal in shape, that it fulfilled the need for someplace to put his ashes.

Then the guest asked, "So Johnny, How much would you be willing to spend for a brown octagonal ashtray like that one?"

"I don't know," said Johnny. "Maybe $20."

"Sold!" said the greatest salesman.

The sales concept behind this interchange is understanding what the customer needs. The secret lies in persuading the customer to state his own needs and then getting him to sell himself. After that, closing becomes a natural progression.

4. **Asking for the order.** You would think this would be obvious, wouldn't you? It's amazing, though, how many salespeople miss the close because they don't even ask. Usually, they're reluctant to ask because they're afraid the customer will say no. But guess what? You hardly ever get a flat no. What you get is an objection. And when you get an objection, you get the opportunity to ask questions, find out the reason for the objection, change what you're doing, and present your solution in a better way. Then, when you've heard the objection and discovered the solution, you can simply say, "Why don't we go ahead with this?"

The first close I ever tried was, "Would you like to put 15 percent down on that, or is 10 percent easier?" The funny thing is, it worked, because without even realizing it, I had established rapport, formed a relationship, discovered the customer's needs, and asked for the order. And I guarantee you, even if I just said, "Why don't we just go ahead with this," it probably would have worked too. Because it doesn't matter if you use the Ben Franklin, alternative choice, right angle, left hook close—if you can't just outright say, "let's go ahead with this," then you better examine all the skills we discussed to earn the right to close in the first place. If you don't build the foundation, the sale is being built on sand and it won't stand.

Follow-Through

According to the definition in *Webster's New World Dictionary, Second Edition*, the term *follow-through* means "the act of continuing an undertaking to completion, to its natural end." But just what is considered the "natural end" of a sale? Is it when the sale is closed? Not if you're looking for repeat business. For most people, selling requires constant cultivation; in order to keep your relationships growing you've got to look at each one and ask yourself, "What other related actions can I take today to strengthen this connection and move it towards a natural end (or at least the next natural level)?"

Most people think that follow-through is a system to ensure that everything gets done. That's only part of it. Follow-through is what you do to ensure that you build the strongest, longest-lasting relationships possible. Your enthusiasm and determination to succeed—attached to benefits for your customers—are the fuel that help you take the most effective steps to follow up and follow through.

After the close of every sale you should be asking yourself, "What can I realistically do to move this sale and this relationship to the next level?" You can—and should—take the standard follow-up steps: When you attend a meeting, follow it up with a letter summarizing the main points of your discussion; send thank-you notes for appointments, demonstrations, orders, and referrals; send articles of personal and professional interest; and find new ways to connect with your customers.

But these steps should not be taken blindly. They must be taken while considering the benefits. Effective follow-through is not just providing additional information; it's discovering steps that you can take to increase or enhance your customer's growth and how you can help build his business beyond this particular sale. A robot can perform standard follow-up tasks. Effective follow-up means finding out what *you* can bring to this relationship that someone else might not have. Think about who your customer is, what he needs most, and how you can best meet that need. Then your follow-through will come naturally. You'll be following his agenda—not yours—and providing a valuable benefit.

The Sales Cycle Checklist

Recently, somebody asked me about my early sales experiences. When I thought about being new to sales, I remembered one company that gave me a laminated card with questions printed front and back. These questions served as a constant reminder of what I needed to do before, during, and after the sale.

Although I no longer carry this card around, it was a great tool to help me learn the business of sales, and served as great reminder over the years. We all need reminders now and then, no matter how skilled we are. So here is a list of questions, similar to the ones printed on that card years ago, that can take you through the sales cycle, step-by-step.

When prospecting, did I:

❑ Find the best possible resources for locating new customers?

❑ Cultivate the gatekeeper whenever possible?

❑ Start early and stay late—calling potential customers during off hours?

❑ Find creative ways to find new propsects?

❑ Stay persistent and tenacious in trying to make contact with hard-to-see executives?

When qualifying, did I:

❑ Ask, "Is there anybody, besides yourself, who might be involved in the decision-making process?"

❑ Ask, "What does a vendor need to do to earn your business?"

❑ Find out how and why the decision was made to purchase the present product or service?

❑ Find out what the time frame is?

❑ Find out if funds have been allocated?

❑ Uncover the specific needs?

❑ Ask all relevant qualifying questions?

❑ Have them go into depth by using phrases such as: "tell me about...," "describe...," and "elaborate..."?

During the presentation/demonstration, did I:

❑ Prepare thoroughly?

❑ Follow the four Ts?

❑ Link the presentation to the prospect's key needs?

❑ Speak from the heart and not from a script?

❑ Present with passion and pizzazz?

❑ Concentrate on getting my message across rather than relying too much on technology?

When closing, did I:

❑ Earn the right to close by following all previous steps in the sales cycle?

❑ Build rapport?

❑ Form a relationship?

❑ Do a thorough needs analysis?

❑ Ask for the order?

For follow-through, did I:

❑ Send a thank you letter for the appointment, presentation, order, and so on?

❑ Send a summary memo?

❑ Establish an ongoing relationship?

❑ Discover what unique value I can bring to the table to meet this customer's ongoing needs?

No one should be asking these questions by rote. It's not a script that could or should be followed for every sale, but it is a great structure to keep in mind. Take a hint from a popular infomercial I'm sure you've seen—the one where the famous pitch man Ron Popeil tells you to "set it... and forget it." Learn this step-by-step procedure—and then forget it. Pull it out when you're puzzled by why you didn't make a sale. Maybe there's something you forgot to do that you should have remembered!

Chapter 11
ACTION STEPS FOR OVERCOMING OBSTACLES

Objections are the obstacles that every salesperson encounters on the way to a close. There is no way to get around this fact. But there are ways to keep yourself motivated when obstacles seem to be hitting you hard. That's what this final chapter is about—motivation for those times when it seems that you're facing more obstacles, setbacks, and adversity than usual.

There's an old saying that goes, "Into every life a little rain must fall." Some lives are flooded with adversity; others have sprinkles of it here and there. But everyone goes through it. The purpose of this chapter is to help you understand that the obstacles pushing us back when we're trying to go forward are not only testing us; they're also giving us an opportunity to learn great lessons. Challenges present us with the greatest opportunities. How you deal with adversity depends on how you view it, how you react, and how you move in the case of rejection and failure.

If you're taking actions that present no challenges, you're not going after anything important. Everything worth having involves some sort of risk. If you want to achieve something big, you're going to run into obstacles that are just as large. The following action steps can help you face those challenges and come out wiser, stronger, and happier.

Action Step Number 1:
Don't Let Illusion Cloud Your Perception

William Blake once said, "If the doors of perception were cleansed everything would appear to man as it is, infinite." Most of the barriers that we come across in life are illusions. We are stopped by the words and thoughts of others. "You can't do that." "No one has ever done that before." "You can't get there from here." We're stopped by these barriers that have no walls, no railings, no barricades, no blockades, and no perimeters. The only true barrier is our own perception.

> We must look for the opportunity in every difficulty instead of being paralyzed at the thought of the difficulty in every opportunity.
>
> —Walter E. Cole

Most of the barriers in sales, we create ourselves. We think we're not experienced, not knowledgeable enough, not good enough. Once we let that into our minds, our perception of reality is not clear. The customer senses when we feel that way.

The only thing that can break through that perception is action. When the doors of perception are cleansed, when the illusions are washed away, limitless possibilities come into view. You can get there from here. You might have to take a different route than the one you had originally planned on taking. You might have to take a risk, perhaps fall on your face a few times. But the further you go, the fewer barriers you encounter. And the only way to discover this truth is to make the journey yourself.

Action Step Number 2:
Challenge Yourself Every Day

Push yourself a little farther every day. Challenge yourself to call on people so that you have more practice in qualifying and handling objections and learn from every experience. No book can come close to the reality of the action that you take. Build up as much activity as possible so that you keep learning through doing.

If we keep our dreams only in our minds, they remain vague and have a "some day" quality about them. When we write them down, it's almost as if we tell ourselves, "Okay. Now you've made a commitment. I dare you to follow through on it."

It's possible to let dreams go by, but it's difficult to ignore a challenge. Think about times when someone dared you to do something. It probably spurred you on, got your blood pumping and gave your brain a jump start. A challenge creates energy, and energy enables us to take action. Challenges get us thinking of ways to go beyond our present limitations (real or imagined). When we're heading into the unknown, our adrenaline starts flowing. We get "hungrier." We become more focused. The stakes become higher.

When you challenge yourself to achieve specific goals, you pull yourself forward. You may not make it every time; there are times when you will experience setbacks and failures. But that only makes the challenge greater. You are being given an opportunity to begin again and perhaps find a better route. Every challenge is a learning experience. You don't learn from the things you already know how to do. You learn from striving, stretching, reaching, and traveling roads you have not gone down before.

Children know this instinctively. Children face challenges every day; they start off knowing nothing, so everything is a challenge to them. Kids have an insatiable curiosity—they are seldom afraid to try new things. And the joy they experience when they have mastered even the smallest skill is immediately apparent. There is nothing sweeter than the sound of a child's exuberant laughter when he first learns to take a few steps, to catch a ball, or to say a new word. We must learn to recapture this joy in small accomplishments. You don't have to wait until you reach your goal to be proud of yourself. Pat yourself on the back for doing research on a company or industry you'd like to break into. Feel good about staying a half hour later at work to make more phone calls. Enjoy the fact that you closed one more sale this week than you did the week before.

Feel good about your accomplishments, then move on. If you have stayed half an hour later to make calls, try staying an hour later the next time. Set your goal to close two more sales next week. Use the pride and energy you get from each small accomplishment to fuel the next steps forward.

Action Step Number 3: Find Problems to Solve That Others Run Away From

People who always look for the easy way out don't reap the big rewards. Those who are willing to step in when others say the road is too difficult are those who truly succeed. A friend of mine was doing fairly well as a sales representative for an insurance company. Then he was moved to another state. He left behind all his old leads and contacts. He knew it could take a long time to build up his clientele in the new territory, so he decided to take on all the complainers and problem customers he could find. The other sales reps were happy to unload their difficult clients, those who were constantly dissatisfied or were not paying their premiums.

My friend sat down with these customers and listened to their problems and complaints. He found ways to solve them. He helped these customers with their insurance needs, and as a result, he helped himself get ahead. He took on the customers no one else wanted, and he soon became the number one insurance sales rep in the country. He did not run away from problems, he embraced them instead. He saw problems not as obstacles, but rather as opportunities for growth.

Action Step Number 4: If You Come to a Barrier You Can't Pass Through, Recreate Yourself

Some barriers are impenetrable. If you keep trying the same old way to get past them, you will inevitably fail. So you must find new ways. Create something new. Discover new passages. You must adapt to the situation in which you find yourself. If you keep hitting your head against the wall trying to get a project done, it may be that you need to change your direction and go around the wall instead.

Here's an example: If I'm trying to get business from a company I've never worked with before, I always call on the person at the top—the owner, the president, or the CEO. Sometimes I get through, but other times I get nowhere. I could give up on that company. Instead, I contact people in other areas of the company, perhaps a top distributor for that organization, and make myself known to them. That person can then refer me back to the top brass. If I find that I have reached a dead end, I take what I have learned from this experience, and move on.

It is the scientific approach to life. Scientists are faced with a particular problem and search for ways to solve it. When they are trying to discover a new drug, they don't expect to come up with the answer on their first try. They try many different avenues. They know that they will take three steps forward and two steps back and that they will come upon many detours along the way. But they keep recreating the drug until they find the right combination of chemicals. And, as they're experimenting, they take notice of ways that they're findings can be applied in other areas as well. A drug that is being designed to ease arthritis pain, for instance, may be found to have properties that reduce the pain of migraine headaches.

There are three ways to deal with the barriers you face. When you come upon a brick wall, you can:

1. **Climb it.** Look for toeholds. Build a ladder. Ask to stand on someone else's shoulders.

2. **Go around it.** Keep moving until you come to the end and travel around the wall. Or find another entry, a tunnel or bridge that will get you to the same destination via a different route.

3. **Go through it.** At least make the attempt. You might find out that the wall is only a facade—an illusion that you have constructed out of fear. If it's not a facade, you might not be able to penetrate the wall. But during the attempt, you will discover what the wall is made of, how thick and tall it is, and what has happened to others who have tried to pass it. Then, the next time you come upon this wall (or one like it), you'll have a head start at getting through. And last, but not least, someone on the other side may see your struggle and decide to give you a hand.

So as you come up against a barrier in your life, look for every possible way to climb it, get around it, or go through it. Adapt, adjust, and recreate; adapt, adjust, and recreate again; and eventually you'll come out stronger and wiser on the other side.

Action Step Number 5:
Don't Forget Your Past Rejections

Dwelling on the past does nothing but slow you down. Learning from it, however, can spur you forward. If you were rejected, ask yourself why. Is there anything you can use to make your next attempt more successful? Even if you feel you were wrongly rejected (and don't we all?), use your anger constructively. There is an incredible amount of energy that goes into anger, and you can choose the way that energy gets utilized. It can eat away at your confidence, willpower, and determination. It can tempt you

> 66 I do not fear failure. I only fear the 'slowing down' of the engine inside me which is pounding, saying, 'Keep going, someone must be on top, why not you?'
> —George S. Patton, U.S. general 99

to take revenge against those who wronged you. Or you can turn it into a positive force that propels you forward and keeps you going past all obstacles.

When you succeed, after everyone has said you would fail, that is the best revenge. It's revenge without hurting anyone. If you let those people stop you or bring you down, then they have won. If you succeed despite them, then you have won. So don't dwell on your rejections, but don't forget about them either. Use them to push you on to new heights.

163

Action Step Number 6: Get Mad and Get Moving

There are some things that are difficult to teach, some things that you just have to learn for yourself. This is one of them: Rejection and failure are just a part of the game. It happens to everyone, and you can let it bring you down and stop you dead, or you can let it energize you to move to even greater heights.

When people put you down, don't believe them! Get mad and get moving. They don't know who you are. They don't know what you're capable of doing. They have no power over you. You have the power to prove them right or prove them wrong. If you want to prove them right, do nothing. Give up your dreams. Stop what you're doing. Feel sorry for yourself.

But if you want to prove them wrong, keep moving. Take action. Use that rejection as fuel to keep you motivated. Just understand that life is never a smooth ride that comes with constant encouragement and approval. It is a bumpy road we travel, and all along the way there are people putting up roadblocks and detours. That doesn't mean you turn around and go home.

Let negative situations energize you instead of pulling you down. There will always be people who tell you that your dreams are impossible. They try to convince you that you don't have the ability or the talent to reach your goals. They say, "That's not the way things are done." They say, "What you're trying to accomplish is so difficult, you might as well give up now."

You can believe those people, or you can turn that negative energy into the driving force that pushes you forward. Create a vision of those naysayers in your mind, and then use that vision as a springboard to prove them wrong. Challenge yourself to show them what you really can do.

Alan Schonberg is the founder and chairman of Management Recruiters International, the world's largest search firm. He has to deal with rejection all the time, both for himself and for clients he's trying to place. "Rejection is hard for everyone," he says, "but the first thing I always consider is 'Who the hell is rejecting me? What basis do they have to reject me? Are they right?' If they're right, I'd better make some changes. And if they're wrong, it's their mistake and their loss."

Action Step Number 7:
Eliminate the "Option" of Failure

When the NASA ground crew admitted that failure to return the Apollo 13 crew to Earth was "not an option," they eliminated it as a possibility. They committed themselves so totally to that statement that they were able to focus solely on what they could accomplish.

When you make this kind of commitment, you stop your brain from accepting excuses. Without this commitment, your brain will accept excuses, you will waver. You will say the things we all tell ourselves when things get tough: "I'm not sure I can do this," or "I could try this, but what's the point? It will never work." If failure is not an option, you will try all kinds of things in the pursuit of success, because you have no choice but to press forward."

Action Step Number 8:
Life Is Too Serious to Be Taken Seriously

When stress is at its worst, when the tension is unbearable, when things are looking bleak, it's time to lighten up. The curative powers of humor are incredible. Sometimes humor allows you to fly past it all and to put things in perspective. It's good to laugh at yourself, and to make others laugh as well. Take time for levity. If you hear a good joke, pass it on. It's a great way to network. Take a short break during the day and call someone who can use some cheering up. Or send

> "I never did a day's work in my life. It was all fun.
>
> —Thomas Edison, inventor"

an e-mail. That way, you won't interrupt someone's busy schedule, but you can still brighten his or her day.

Laughter is not only good for health; it usually lets you see things from a different light. Why are comedians funny? It's not that they see different things than we do, it's that they see things differently. Listen to your favorite comedians and take a hint from the way they look at life. The best of them take the simple things we do every day in life, the flaws and foibles that make us human, and make us laugh at the absurdity of it all.

But we don't always need comedians to make us laugh at life. We must learn to laugh at ourselves, and to count our blessings. Humor can help you deal with even the most serious of situations. When you look at others who are in truly dire straits, it helps to put your own worries in perspective.

Studies have shown that children laugh anywhere from 100 to 400 times a day. The average adult laughs about 4 times a day. That's sad. Laughter is the best stress-reliever known to man. It opens our creative juices. People want to be around other people who are happy and laughing.

A salesperson I know recently told me the secret of his success: He's a happy person. He admitted that he didn't have the greatest sales techniques in the world. "That's what gets me in the door and gets me a lot of business," he said.

"If people are in a bad mood, I try to turn them around, to make them feel better. I try to lighten up their day. Once I do that, everything else follows. I don't make every sale, but people remember me and welcome me back again."

INDEX

ABOUT THE AUTHOR

Barry Farber is the author of 10 books (several of which have been translated into 18 foreign languages) on sales, management, and personal achievement, including *Diamond Power, Superstar Sales Secrets, Revised Edition*, and *Superstar Sales Manager's Secrets, Revised Edition*. He is also the president of three successful companies: Farber Training Systems, a sales and management training company; The Diamond Group, a literary agency; and Profound Products Inc., a company that creates and markets innovative products.

Well-known as a public speaker and writer, as well as a television guest and host, Barry is also a monthly columnist for *Entrepreneur* magazine, host of *Selling Power Live*, and one of the nation's highest rated speakers on sales, leadership, and motivation. He is a black belt in Tae Kwon Do and is currently training in aikido and jujitsu. He has won awards at state, regional, and national levels in weapons competitions with a six-foot bo staff. Barry received a first-place ranking in state and regional competitions and achieved second place in a National Karate Tournament, black belt division. He often uses his martial arts experience to tie into his messages on sales, marketing, and success. For more information about Barry and his products, visit *www.barryfarber.com*.